INTERNATIONAL NARCOTICS CONTROL BOARD

Precursors

and chemicals frequently used in the illicit manufacture of narcotic drugs and psychotropic substances

Report of the International Narcotics Control Board for 2015 on the Implementation of Article 12 of the United Nations Convention against Illicit Traffic in Narcotic Drugs and Psychotropic Substances of 1988

UNITED NATIONS
New York, 2016

E/INCB/2015/4

UNITED NATIONS PUBLICATION
Sales No. E.16.XI.4
ISBN: 978-92-1-148284-3
eISBN: 978-92-1-057749-6

Publishing production: English, Publishing and Library Section, United Nations Office at Vienna.

Foreword

In the run-up to the special session of the General Assembly on the world drug problem to be held in April 2016, I am pleased to present the International Narcotics Control Board's 2015 report on precursors.

The 2015 report, like the previous reports, highlights the dynamics of chemical diversion control, in terms of geographical aspects and in terms of the chemicals themselves. It also highlights, once again, the successes that can be achieved when Governments work together, share information and engage in joint action. The Board's initiatives, platforms and networks, such as the Precursor Task Force, Project Prism and Project Cohesion and the related communication platform known as the Precursors Incident Communication System (PICS), provide a framework in which Governments have achieved significant and tangible results at the global level.

The report also covers the Board's Pre-Export Notification Online (PEN Online) system. In the nearly 10 years since it came into existence, PEN Online has become the most effective tool used by Governments to monitor, and communicate about matters related to, international trade in scheduled chemicals worldwide. The Board is pleased to have been able to launch an enhanced version of the system in 2015.

At this point in the run-up to the special session of the General Assembly to be held in 2016, a realistic assessment of the situation is needed. The international precursor control regime has made significant progress in monitoring legitimate international trade in a defined set of precursor chemicals to prevent them from being diverted into illicit channels. However, drugs are still being manufactured using non-scheduled chemicals, and they are emerging in a seemingly unlimited number of new forms or with new modifications.

The Board is convinced that the current challenges require efforts that go beyond the letter of article 12 of the United Nations Convention against Illicit Traffic in Narcotic Drugs and Psychotropic Substances of 1988. The Board is also convinced that the time has come to take new paths. First steps have already been made by some, including at the regional level, moving away from defined lists of controlled chemicals towards innovative generic approaches, such as the concept of "immediate" precursors, or providing a framework for law enforcement action when there is evidence that a substance is intended for use in the illicit manufacture of drugs. Voluntary private-public partnerships, as the present report shows, are also among those tools that can effectively and proactively prevent the diversion of any chemical at its source.

On behalf of the Board, I therefore wish to invite all Governments and interested regional and international organizations to continue to work with each other, the Board and its secretariat, to identify, agree on and implement the necessary practical framework that will enable the international community, collectively, to meet the challenges ahead. In doing so, we should build on the existing tools and mechanisms and the lessons learned to date, refining them where necessary, but we should also be unafraid to explore new ground. The Board is ready for this journey and ready to assist when requested.

Werner **Sipp**
President of the International
Narcotics Control Board

Preface

The United Nations Convention against Illicit Traffic in Narcotic Drugs and Psychotropic Substances of 1988 provides that the International Narcotics Control Board shall submit a report annually to the Commission on Narcotic Drugs on the implementation of article 12 of the Convention and that the Commission shall periodically review the adequacy and propriety of Tables I and II of the Convention.

In addition to its annual report and other technical publications (on narcotic drugs and psychotropic substances), the Board has prepared its report on the implementation of article 12 of the 1988 Convention in accordance with the following provisions contained in article 23 of the Convention:

1. The Board shall prepare an annual report on its work containing an analysis of the information at its disposal and, in appropriate cases, an account of the explanations, if any, given by or required of Parties, together with any observations and recommendations which the Board desires to make. The Board may make such additional reports as it considers necessary. The reports shall be submitted to the [Economic and Social] Council through the Commission which may make such comments as it sees fit.

2. The reports of the Board shall be communicated to the Parties and subsequently published by the Secretary-General. The Parties shall permit their unrestricted distribution.

Contents

---

[*] The annexes are not included in the printed version of the present report but are available in the CD-ROM version and in the version on the website of the International Narcotics Control Board (www.incb.org).

Explanatory notes

The boundaries and names shown and the designations used on the maps in this publication do not imply official endorsement or acceptance by the United Nations.

The designations employed and the presentation of the material in this publication do not imply the expression of any opinion whatsoever on the part of the Secretariat of the United Nations concerning the legal status of any country, territory, city or area or of its authorities, or concerning the delimitation of its frontiers or boundaries.

Countries and areas are referred to by the names that were in official use at the time the relevant data were collected.

Multiple government sources of data were used to generate the present report, including the information provided each year on form D (information on substances frequently used in the illicit manufacture of narcotic drugs and psychotropic substances), notifications via the Pre-Export Notification Online (PEN Online) system, the Precursors Incident Communication System (PICS) and other official communications with competent national authorities. Unless otherwise specified, data provided on form D are referred to by the calendar year to which they apply; the cut-off date for reporting the data is 30 June of the following year. The reporting period for data from the PEN Online system and PICS is from 1 November 2014 to 1 November 2015, unless otherwise specified. In cases in which PEN Online data are used for multiple years, calendar years are used. Additional information was also provided through regional and international partner organizations, as indicated in the report.

Reference to "tons" is to metric tons, unless otherwise stated.

The following abbreviations have been used in the present report:

APAAN	*alpha*-phenylacetoacetonitrile
CICAD	Inter-American Drug Abuse Control Commission
GBL	*gamma*-butyrolactone
GHB	*gamma*-hydroxybutyric acid
INCB	International Narcotics Control Board
INTERPOL	International Criminal Police Organization
LSD	lysergic acid diethylamide
MDMA	3,4-methylenedioxymethamphetamine
3,4-MDP-2-P	3,4-methylenedioxyphenyl-2-propanone
P-2-P	1-phenyl-2-propanone
PEN Online	Pre-Export Notification Online
PICS	Precursors Incident Communication System
PMA	*para*-methoxy-*alpha*-methylphenethylamine
PMMA	*para*-methoxymethamphetamine
UNODC	United Nations Office on Drugs and Crime

Summary

The International Narcotics Control Board (INCB), in cooperation with the United Nations Office on Drugs and Crime and as a contribution to the special session of the General Assembly on the world drug problem to be held in 2016, convened in Bangkok in April 2015 an international conference entitled Precursor Chemicals and New Psychoactive Substances. The conference participants adopted an outcome document on addressing pertinent global challenges in precursor control, new psychoactive substances and related international cooperation.[a] INCB also launched at the conference a document to provide practical guidance to support Governments' implementation of the *Guidelines for a Voluntary Code of Practice for the Chemical Industry*, prepared by the Board in 2009.

Public-private partnerships and the work of INCB in this area are also given special focus in the present report, reflecting the strong belief on the part of the Board and many Governments in the merits and potential of this concept as one of the key components for addressing present and future challenges in precursor control.

One of these challenges, identified on the basis of information provided by Governments on form D for 2014, which is also evident through the Precursors Incident Communication System (PICS), is the continued diversification in illicit drug manufacture, in particular illicit synthetic drug manufacture. This includes chemicals available off the shelf, as well as a number of unusual chemicals that may be made on demand with a view to circumventing existing controls ("designer" precursors). Although the quantities are mostly still small, a new trend that may be unfolding is the use of benzaldehyde and nitroethane, or the subsequent intermediate 1-phenyl-2-nitropropene, in illicit manufacture of both amphetamine and methamphetamine. Because monomethylamine had been identified as a key chemical used in the illicit manufacture of various drugs and precursors, INCB conducted an operation under Project Prism targeting that chemical, its supply and its distribution, with a view to identifying suspicious transactions.

Chemicals that had been prominent in previous periods, such as *alpha*-phenylacetoacetonitrile (APAAN) and esters of phenylacetic acid, continued to be seized during the reporting period, although the seizures were typically smaller than before and occurred less frequently at international borders, suggesting that international controls (particularly regarding APAAN) and the measures introduced in the countries concerned, and in the countries from which, consignments had originated in the past, are having the desired effects.

In 2015, diversion from domestic distribution channels continued to be a major source of substances used in illicit drug manufacture, in particular acids and solvents listed in Table II of the United Nations Convention against Illicit Traffic in Narcotic Drugs and Psychotropic Substances of 1988. Likewise, domestic sources were often used to obtain ephedrine and pseudoephedrine, potassium permanganate and acetic anhydride. During the reporting period, the Governments of several countries, including Afghanistan, China and Nigeria, took measures to identify the extent of domestic diversions and identify sources and modi operandi. Several Governments have strengthened or fine-tuned existing controls over precursor chemicals, as highlighted in chapter II of the present report.

In 2015, a number of discrepancies between the supply (availability) of drug end products and seizures of the precursors of those drugs became more apparent. They relate to almost all drugs and precursors, in different regions, and include, for

---

[a] https://www.incb.org/documents/Publications/PressRelease/PR2015/Outcome_document_FINAL_rev02.pdf.

example, the continued lack of information about the sources of chemicals feeding the illicit manufacture of heroin from opium poppy grown in Afghanistan. Similar considerations apply to countries in South-East Asia, in particular Myanmar, the country with the second-largest total area under illicit opium poppy cultivation and the second-largest potential opium production; and to the situation in West Asia regarding Captagon. Long-standing conflicts and political instability in many such regions complicate implementation of the necessary action.

In terms of the core parameters used to define the functioning of the international precursor control system, no State became a party to the 1988 Convention in 2015, so there continue to be nine States that have yet to accede to the Convention. Bangladesh and the Sudan invoked article 12, paragraph 10 (a), of the Convention, making it mandatory for exporting countries to send pre-export notifications prior to a planned export, and Burundi registered with the Board's Pre-Export Notification Online (PEN Online) system, bringing to 151 the total number of countries registered with the system. PEN Online continued to prove that it plays an essential role as an effective means of preventing the diversion of precursor chemicals, with an increasing number of communications between the authorities of importing and exporting countries having been recorded within the PEN Online framework, resulting in the stopping of numerous suspicious shipments in international trade. A PEN Online system upgrade was launched in 2015.

To remind Governments of the basic kinds of action they could take to enhance international precursor control, the present report summarizes minimum action in three areas: (a) international trade monitoring through the PEN Online system; (b) international cooperation under Project Prism and Project Cohesion; and (c) sharing information about precursor incidents through PICS. The report also highlights the value of forensic analysis, especially in the form of drug characterization and impurity profiling studies, to support precursor control measures by improving knowledge of the chemicals actually being used in illicit drug manufacture and their sources. The Board encourages enhanced international cooperation in this area.

I. Introduction

1. The present report has been prepared by the International Narcotics Control Board (INCB) pursuant to the provisions of the United Nations Convention against Illicit Traffic in Narcotic Drugs and Psychotropic Substances of 1988.[1] In this report, as in all the reports on precursors issued since 2011, one precursor-related theme is addressed in more depth: in chapter IV below, the Board reviews the merits and potential of public-private partnerships to prevent the diversion of chemicals.

2. Substantive reporting begins in chapter II with information on action taken by Governments and INCB pursuant to article 12 of the 1988 Convention. It includes statistics on adherence to the Convention and reporting to the Board, legislation and control measures, as well as the utilization of the Board's Pre-Export Notification Online (PEN Online) system. Chapter II concludes with an overview of the activities and achievements of the two international initiatives of INCB addressing chemicals used in the illicit manufacture of amphetamine-type stimulants (Project Prism) and cocaine and heroin (Project Cohesion), including the status of utilization of the Precursors Incident Communication System (PICS).

3. Chapter III continues with an overview of information on the legitimate trade in individual precursor chemicals, as well as major trends in their trafficking and illicit use. The analysis includes information on the most relevant cases involving suspicious or stopped shipments of precursor chemicals, diversions or attempted diversions of those chemicals from legitimate trade, and seizures of those chemicals. Specific recommendations and conclusions are highlighted throughout the report to facilitate concrete action to be taken by Governments with the aim of preventing such diversions. Overall conclusions are presented in chapter V, following the thematic chapter on public-private partnerships.

4. As in the past, annexes I-XI to the report provide updated statistics and practical information to assist competent national authorities in carrying out their functions. The annexes are available only in the CD-ROM version of the report and in the version on the INCB website.

II. Action taken by Governments and the International Narcotics Control Board

A. Adherence to the 1988 Convention

5. As at 1 November 2015, the 1988 Convention had been ratified, acceded to or approved by 189 States and formally confirmed by the European Union (extent of competence: article 12). There have been no changes in this regard since the publication of the Board's 2014 report on precursors, leaving nine States — five in Oceania, three in Africa and one in West Asia — that have yet to become parties to the Convention (see annex I).[2] The geographical proximity of some of the non-parties to illicit drug-manufacturing areas makes those States vulnerable to precursor trafficking. **Therefore, the Board urges those nine States to implement the provisions of article 12 and accede to the 1988 Convention without further delay.**

B. Reporting to the Board pursuant to article 12 of the 1988 Convention

6. Pursuant to article 12, paragraph 12, of the 1988 Convention, it is mandatory for States parties to submit annually to INCB information on: the seized amounts of substances in Tables I and II of the Convention and, when known, their origin; any substance not included in Table I or II which is identified as having been used in illicit manufacture of narcotic drugs or psychotropic substances; and methods of diversion and illicit manufacture. Such information is to be submitted through form D by 30 June of the following year at the latest, although the Board encourages States parties to submit the information by an earlier date (30 April) to facilitate the analysis of and follow-up to the information provided.

7. As at 1 November 2015, a total of 117 States and territories had submitted form D for 2014, a significantly lower submission rate than for the past 10 years (see annex VII for details). About 5 per cent of the submitting States and territories used older versions of form D, thus providing an incomplete set of information.

8. The Sudan and Zambia resumed their submission of form D after having failed to do so for a number of years. Some States parties to the 1988 Convention (Burundi, Gabon and Marshall Islands) have never submitted form D

---

[1] United Nations, *Treaty Series*, vol. 1582, No. 27627.

[2] Equatorial Guinea, Kiribati, Palau, Papua New Guinea, Solomon Islands, Somalia, South Sudan, State of Palestine and Tuvalu.

to the Board, while other States parties[3] have not done so in the past five years. A total of 79 States parties failed to submit to the Board a report for 2014.[4] As in previous years, only a small proportion (47, or 24 per cent) of Governments submitted the form before 30 June, while others failed to report altogether, submitted a blank form or provided only partial information. This situation continues to have an impact on the Board's analysis of regional and global precursor patterns and trends. **The Board urges all States parties to comply with their reporting obligations under the 1988 Convention. States are also reminded to use the latest version of form D, which is available on the INCB website in Arabic, Chinese, English, French, Russian and Spanish, and submit it within the requested time frame.**

9.   A total of 56 Governments reported on form D for 2014 seizures of substances in Table I or II of the 1988 Convention;[5] and 33 also reported seizures of substances not in Table I or II. The reporting of information on methods of diversion and illicit manufacture or on stopped shipments continues to be limited, although it is precisely those details that would help to prevent similar incidents from happening elsewhere. Only 21 per cent of all those submitting the form included information on methods of diversion and illicit manufacture. The Board is concerned that significant seizures of precursor chemicals included by some Governments in their national reports or in their official conference presentations are not reported on form D. **The Board once again wishes to remind Governments effecting seizures to provide on form D complete and comprehensive data, including, where known, the** origin of seized substances and data on the use of non-scheduled chemicals and methods of diversion and illicit manufacture.

C. Legislation and control measures

10.   In accordance with the provisions of article 12 of the 1988 Convention and the relevant resolutions of the General Assembly, the Economic and Social Council and the Commission on Narcotic Drugs, Governments are requested to adopt and implement national control measures to effectively monitor the movement of precursor chemicals. In addition, Governments are requested to further strengthen existing precursor control measures should any weaknesses be identified.

11.   Following the tightening of controls over ephedra in 2013, Chinese authorities conducted a survey on the management of ephedra cultivation in Chifeng, in the Inner Mongolia Autonomous Region of China. Authorities also proceeded with the establishment of precursor chemical industry associations at the provincial level; inspections of precursor chemical manufacturers and pharmacies in the provinces were conducted.[6]

12.   In January 2015, resolution 0001/2015 adopted in Colombia resulted in controls being tightened for a range of precursor chemicals. For example, controls were established throughout the entire country for transactions involving any amount of potassium permanganate (rather than transactions involving more than 5 kg). The same "zero threshold" applies to transactions involving acetic anhydride, hydrochloric acid and sulphuric acid.

13.   In February 2015, in response to a Project Prism/Project Cohesion alert, the authorities of the Lao People's Democratic Republic informed INCB about the inclusion of alpha-phenylacetoacetonitrile (APAAN) in table I of the national legislation governing the list of narcotic drugs, psychotropic substances and precursors. The Board was also informed that the Government had tightened controls over pseudoephedrine in June 2014.

14.   On 30 June 2015, European Commission delegated regulation No. 2015/1011 of 24 April 2015 and Commission implementing regulation No. 2015/1013 of 25 June 2015 came into effect, repealing and replacing Commission regulation No. 1277/2005. The main changes relate to the possibility of using simplified procedures for pre-export notifications and for export authorizations for medicinal products containing ephedrine or pseudoephedrine and to conditions for granting registration to operators. In addition, procedures were established for granting licences

---

3   Angola, Antigua and Barbuda, Bahamas, Botswana, Cabo Verde, Central African Republic, Comoros, Congo, Djibouti, Dominica, Grenada, Guinea, Lesotho, Libya, Malawi, Mauritania, Niger, Rwanda, Saint Kitts and Nevis, Sierra Leone, Suriname, Swaziland and Tonga.

4   Angola; Antigua and Barbuda; Bahamas; Bahrain; Barbados; Belize; Botswana; Burkina Faso; Burundi; Cabo Verde; Cameroon; Canada; Central African Republic; Chad; Comoros; Congo; Cook Islands; Cuba; Democratic People's Republic of Korea; Djibouti; Dominica; Eritrea; Ethiopia; Fiji; Gabon; Gambia; Grenada; Guinea; Guinea-Bissau; Haiti; Holy See; Honduras; India; Iraq; Kazakhstan; Kenya; Kuwait; Lesotho; Liberia; Libya; Liechtenstein; Madagascar; Malawi; Maldives; Mali; Marshall Islands; Mauritania; Mauritius; Micronesia (Federated States of); Monaco; Mongolia; Morocco; Nauru; New Zealand; Niger; Nigeria; Niue; Norway; Paraguay; Qatar; Rwanda; Saint Kitts and Nevis; Samoa; San Marino; Sao Tome and Principe; Serbia; Seychelles; Sierra Leone; South Africa; Suriname; Swaziland; Syrian Arab Republic; Tajikistan; the former Yugoslav Republic of Macedonia; Togo; Tonga; Ukraine; Vanuatu and Yemen.

5   For details on the reported seizures of those substances, by region, see annex VIII.

6   National Narcotics Control Commission of China, *Annual Report on Drug Control in China 2015* (Beijing, 2015).

and registration to professional users. As at 1 July 2015, after an 18-month transitional period, end users of acetic anhydride had to be registered with their competent national authorities.

15. Also on 1 July 2015, an amendment to the Polish drug act came into force, restricting the sale of over-the-counter medical products containing psychoactive substances, including pseudoephedrine. Such medication may now be sold at pharmacies only in quantities of up to one package. Starting in 2017, any medication containing dosages higher than those to be established by regulation of the Minister of Health of Poland will have to be prescribed by a doctor. Any sale that contravenes the established restrictions will carry a fine of up to 500,000 zlotys (equivalent to more than $125,000).

16. On 1 October 2015, the Mexican Government added four chemicals that could be used in the illicit manufacture of methamphetamine to the list of controlled substances (benzaldehyde, benzyl chloride, nitroethane and nitromethane). A cooperation agreement between the Federal Commission for Protection against Health Risks and the main parts of the chemical industry was signed with a view to defining joint actions to ensure supply of those chemicals for legitimate purposes while preventing diversion into illicit channels. Controls were to be effective after a 90-day transition period following publication in the official gazette.

17. In Australia, an amendment to the Criminal Code Act 1995 is expected to pass into law, removing the requirement of proving that a person who imported or exported a "border controlled precursor"[7] did so with the intention of using it to manufacture a controlled drug or with the belief that another person intended to use the substance to manufacture a controlled drug.

18. In response to a number of cases involving the smuggling of a pharmaceutical preparation containing pseudoephedrine across Europe (see para. 57 below), Turkish authorities tightened controls over the product in question, making it a prescription medication and requiring import and export authorization.

19. Information about individual national systems of authorization applicable to imports and exports of substances in Table I or II of the 1988 Convention, as well as to additional substances under national control, is available on the secure website of INCB, for use by competent national authorities. The INCB information package on the control of precursors is updated whenever new information is made available to the Board.

D. Submission of data on licit trade in, uses of and requirements for precursors

20. Information on the licit trade in and use of substances in Tables I and II of the 1988 Convention is submitted, on a voluntary and confidential basis, to INCB on form D, in accordance with Economic and Social Council resolution 1995/20. Those data enable the Board to assist Governments in preventing diversions by identifying unusual trade patterns and suspicious illicit activity.

21. As at 1 November 2015, 108 countries and territories had provided information on licit trade in substances in Tables I and II of the Convention, and 106 had furnished data on licit uses of and/or requirements for one or more of the substances in Tables I and II (see annex IX). The response rates (as percentages of countries and territories submitting form D) are thus similar to the response rates for the preceding year (when about 90 per cent of countries submitting form D for 2013 provided information on licit trade, uses and/or requirements). The Government of Oman submitted data on licit trade in such substances for the first time in five years. **The Board commends those Governments that provided data on licit trade in, uses of and requirements for substances in Tables I and II of the 1988 Convention and wishes to encourage all other Governments to provide such data with a view to strengthening the existing mechanisms to prevent diversion of those substances.**

E. Annual legitimate requirements for imports of precursors of amphetamine-type stimulants

22. The Commission on Narcotic Drugs, in its resolution 49/3, requested Member States to provide to the Board annual estimates of their legitimate requirements for four substances frequently used in the illicit manufacture of amphetamine-type stimulants — 3,4-methylenedioxyphenyl-2-propanone (3,4-MDP-2-P), pseudoephedrine, ephedrine and 1-phenyl-2-propanone (P-2-P) — and, to the extent possible, estimated requirements for imports of preparations containing those substances, as a means of providing the competent authorities of exporting countries with at least an indication of the needs of importing countries, thus warning about potential oversupply and preventing diversion attempts. The information is provided each year on form D and can also be updated and provided to the Board at any time during the year.

23. As at 1 November 2015, 157 countries and territories had provided estimates for at least one of the

---

[7] A category of precursors defined in Australian law.

above-mentioned substances. Although that number has not changed since INCB published its 2014 report on precursors, the total number of estimates provided by individual countries and territories has increased steadily over the past 10 years (see figure I). The latest estimates submitted by countries and territories are provided in annex II; regular updates are published on the Board's website. The number of competent authorities of exporting countries that have consulted with the Board about the annual legitimate requirements of their trading partners has also steadily increased, thus indicating the value of the estimates and the increased awareness and use of this basic tool. **The Board commends those Governments that make active use of the system of annual legitimate requirements and encourages all other Governments to make better use of this basic tool as both exporters and importers of 3,4-MDP-2-P, pseudoephedrine, ephedrine and P-2-P and preparations containing those substances.**

Figure I. **Number of Governments providing estimates of annual legitimate requirements and total number of estimates provided, 2006-2015**

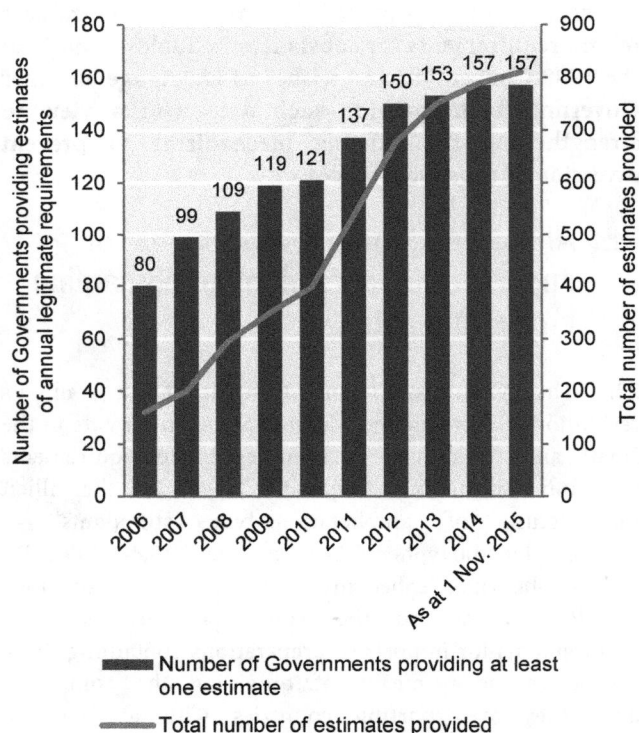

■■■ Number of Governments providing at least one estimate

▬▬ Total number of estimates provided

24. Improvements in national estimate mechanisms and the increased use of annual legitimate requirements are also reflected in the number of Governments regularly reconfirming or revising established estimates. Since the publication of the Board's 2014 report on precursors, about 80 Governments have reconfirmed or updated their estimates for at least one of the substances to reflect changing market conditions, as recommended by the Board. The annual legitimate requirements for the import of pseudoephedrine raw material into the Islamic Republic of Iran have been reduced by almost 70 per cent, from 55 to 17 tons. Other countries that have significantly reduced their annual legitimate requirements for pseudoephedrine raw material include Singapore (from 63 to 35 tons) and Nepal (from 6.5 to 5 tons). The Government of Afghanistan, which reduced its estimates for both ephedrine and pseudoephedrine by 50 per cent in 2014, explained that those requirements should have been for preparations containing those substances and not for raw material.

25. While many countries and territories update their estimates regularly, INCB has noted that some that provided annual legitimate requirements in the past have not done so for more than five years, despite the reminders sent regularly by the Board.[8] The Board continues to be concerned about the relatively high or significantly increasing annual legitimate requirements for various substances and significant year-on-year fluctuations in the estimates submitted by a number of countries. Since the publication of the Board's 2014 report on precursors, this has been true for estimates submitted by the authorities of Bosnia and Herzegovina (increased estimates for ephedrine and pseudoephedrine and preparations containing them), Egypt (an increase in estimates for pseudoephedrine raw material, from 50 to 55 tons), Indonesia (an almost eightfold increase in estimates for pseudoephedrine preparations, from 805 to 6,200 kg) and Israel (an increase from 16 to 3,000 kg in estimates for pseudoephedrine raw material). The Government of the Bolivarian Republic of Venezuela provided, for the first time, estimates for ephedrine preparations (1,000 kg) and pseudoephedrine preparations (2,000 kg). Authorities in Zimbabwe, for the second consecutive year, submitted estimates for P-2-P and 3,4-MDP-2-P of 1,000 litres each, as well as unusually high requirements for several other precursors of amphetamine-type stimulants, including APAAN. The estimates are currently being verified with the authorities. In the meantime, **INCB encourages the authorities of all exporting countries to exercise vigilance in relation to any planned export of P-2-P or 3,4-MDP-2-P to Zimbabwe or elsewhere, considering that those substances are traded and used by a relatively small number of countries.**

---

8 Azerbaijan; Belize; Botswana; Cambodia; China, Macao Special Administrative Region; Guinea; Guinea-Bissau; Madagascar; Malawi; Monaco; Mozambique; Papua New Guinea; Portugal; Russian Federation; Sao Tome and Principe; Solomon Islands; Syrian Arab Republic; Tajikistan and Tristan da Cunha.

26. Governments that reduced their legitimate requirements for ephedrine and pseudoephedrine for 2015 and have now significantly increased the estimates for the same substances for 2016 include the Governments of Pakistan and the United Republic of Tanzania. Pakistan had followed the Board's recommendation and reduced its estimates for 2015 for ephedrine from 22 to 3.3 tons and for pseudoephedrine from 48 to 29.5 tons; for 2016, however, the Government revised those figures significantly upwards, to 12 tons of ephedrine and 48 tons of pseudoephedrine. Similarly, the United Republic of Tanzania, which was among the countries with the most significant reductions in its estimates for 2015, has indicated a 15-fold increase in its estimate for ephedrine preparations. **INCB encourages all Governments to increase their efforts to establish realistic annual legitimate requirements, or review existing ones, and inform the Board accordingly. In preparing their annual legitimate requirements, Governments may wish to consider the** *Guide on Estimating Requirements for Substances under International Control*, **developed by INCB and the World Health Organization, as well as the document entitled "Issues that Governments may consider when determining annual legitimate requirements for ephedrine and pseudoephedrine", available on the Board's website.**

27. As noted in the Board's 2012 report on precursors,[9] a number of Governments have appeared to build in a "safety margin" of significant proportions when estimating their requirements; that is, they actually import significantly less in a given year than what they have estimated to be their annual legitimate requirements for imports. However, only if the estimates are realistic can they serve as a practical tool for preventing the diversion of precursors. **INCB therefore requests all Governments to regularly review their published import requirements, amend them as necessary utilizing the most recent market data and inform the Board of any changes. Such changes can be communicated to the Board at any time and will be reflected in scheduled updates on its official website, as well as in the PEN Online system.**

F. Pre-export notifications and utilization of the Pre-Export Notification Online system

28. Pre-export notifications enable Governments to rapidly identify suspicious transactions in the international trade in substances in Tables I and II of the 1988 Convention, thus preventing diversion of those substances from licit trade channels. Specifically, a pre-export notification makes the competent authorities of an importing country aware of a planned shipment of precursors destined for their territory before the shipment leaves the exporting country, thus enabling them to verify the legitimacy of the transaction and suspend or stop it, as required, in a timely manner. Pursuant to article 12, paragraph 10 (a), of the Convention, Governments of importing countries can make it mandatory for exporting countries to inform them of planned exports of precursors prior to shipping. The invoking of article 12, paragraph 10 (a), of the Convention thus is a fundamental tool for preventing the diversion of precursors from international trade.

29. In 2015, the Governments of Bangladesh and the Sudan invoked article 12, paragraph 10 (a), of the 1988 Convention for all substances in Tables I and II, thus bringing to 109 the number of Governments that have formally requested to receive pre-export notifications (see map 1 and annex X). INCB is concerned that, as indicated in its 2013 report on precursors,[10] in some regions, the majority of Governments have not yet invoked their right to be notified of planned exports of precursors destined for their territory. This applies to Africa (72 per cent), and to Central America and the Caribbean, East and South-East Asia and South Asia (50 per cent each). Although the authorities of a majority of exporting countries issue pre-export notifications for all planned shipments of precursor chemicals, regardless of whether or not the importing country has invoked the article, several exporting countries may not issue such notifications, given the absence of a legal requirement to do so, thus making the importing countries concerned vulnerable to traffickers' diversion attempts. **INCB urges the Governments of those countries to take the necessary steps to invoke the provisions of article 12, paragraph 10 (a), without further delay. Forms to be used for formally requesting to be notified of all shipments of substances in Tables I and II of the 1988 Convention are available from INCB. The Board also wishes to remind the Governments of all countries exporting substances in Tables I and II that it is an obligation to provide pre-export notifications to the authorities of importing countries and territories that have requested them.**

30. The Governments of some countries, including major trading countries, because they do not have under domestic control all substances in Tables I and II of the 1988 Convention, may not be in a position to issue pre-export notifications for shipments of such substances. **Those Governments should take all necessary measures**

---

[9] E/INCB/2012/4, para. 131.

[10] E/INCB/2013/4, table 5.

to comply with their obligations under article 12 of the 1988 Convention with regard to international trade.

31. Pre-export notifications are most efficiently and effectively exchanged via PEN Online, the automated online system for the exchange of pre-export notifications. Since the launch of the PEN Online system in March 2006, the system has become the most effective tool used by related to, international trade in precursor chemicals worldwide. Since the publication of the Board's 2014 report on precursors, Burundi has been added to the list of countries and territories authorized to have access to the PEN Online system (see map 1), bringing to 151 the total number of countries and territories on that list as at 1 November 2015.

Map 1. Governments that have registered with the Pre-Export Notification Online system and those that have invoked article 12, paragraph 10 (a), of the 1988 Convention, requiring pre-export notification for selected substances (as at 1 November 2015)

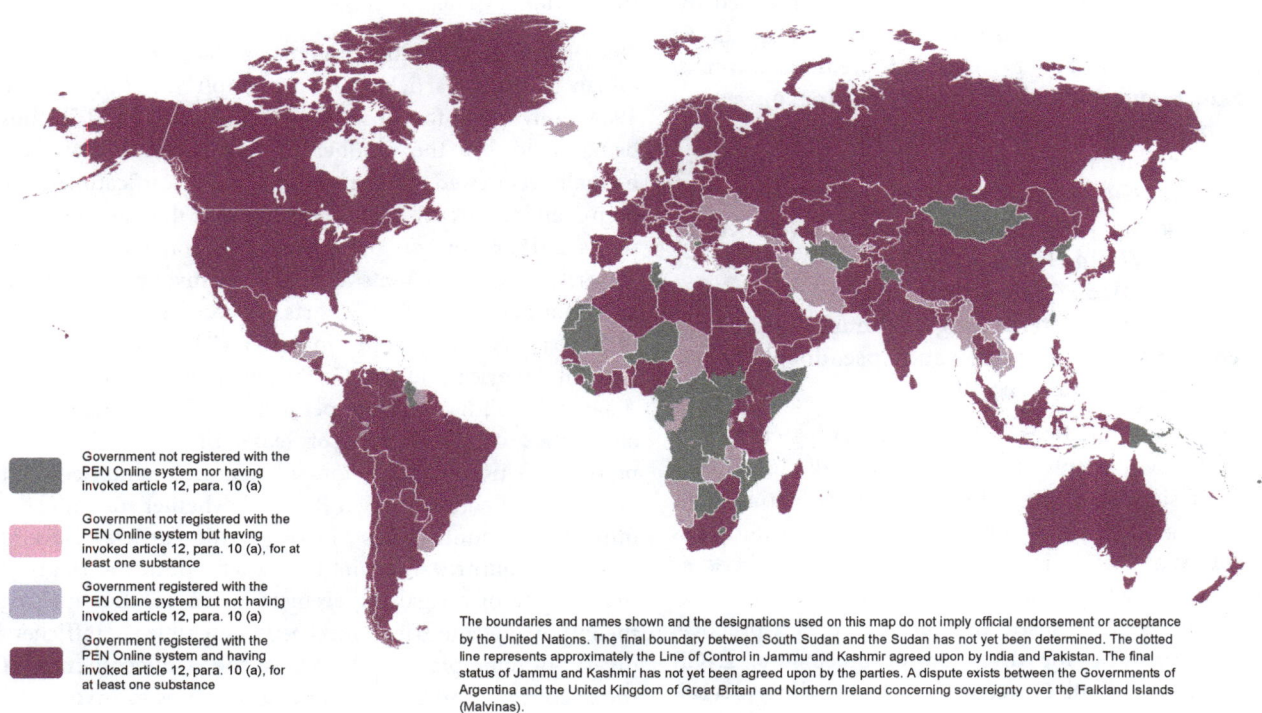

Government not registered with the PEN Online system nor having invoked article 12, para. 10 (a)

Government not registered with the PEN Online system but having invoked article 12, para. 10 (a), for at least one substance

Government registered with the PEN Online system but not having invoked article 12, para. 10 (a)

Government registered with the PEN Online system and having invoked article 12, para. 10 (a), for at least one substance

The boundaries and names shown and the designations used on this map do not imply official endorsement or acceptance by the United Nations. The final boundary between South Sudan and the Sudan has not yet been determined. The dotted line represents approximately the Line of Control in Jammu and Kashmir agreed upon by India and Pakistan. The final status of Jammu and Kashmir has not yet been agreed upon by the parties. A dispute exists between the Governments of Argentina and the United Kingdom of Great Britain and Northern Ireland concerning sovereignty over the Falkland Islands (Malvinas).

32. Since the launch of the PEN Online system over nine years ago, the number of pre-export notifications communicated through the system has increased steadily, averaging more than 2,600 notifications each month in 2015 (see figure II). The increase since January 2014 is related to, among other things, the requirement in States members of the European Union that the export of pharmaceutical preparations containing ephedrine or pseudoephedrine be preceded by an export authorization and a pre-export notification sent to the competent authorities of the country of destination. That became possible as a result of the creation of new specific tariff codes in the combined nomenclature of the European Union, enabling unequivocal identification of pharmaceutical preparations containing ephedrine, pseudoephedrine and norephedrine and thus allowing for better monitoring of trade in those substances. Specific tariff codes for those products were also created in the Harmonized Commodity Description and Coding System of the World Customs Organization and will be applicable starting on 1 January 2017. **INCB commends all Governments that issue pre-export notifications for pharmaceutical preparations containing ephedrine or pseudoephedrine and encourages other Governments to consider, to the extent possible and in accordance with their national legislation, applying to pharmaceutical preparations containing ephedrine or pseudoephedrine control measures that are similar to those applicable to the bulk (raw) substances.**

Figure II. Number of countries and territories authorized to access the Pre-Export Notification Online system and number of pre-export notifications per month, 2006-2015

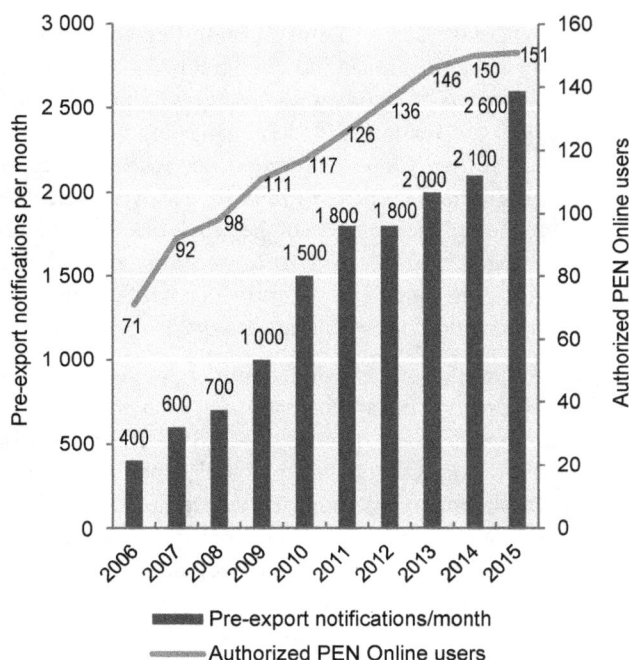

33. While the authorities of major trading countries are registered and actively using the PEN Online system, 46 countries[11] have still not registered with the system. The Board has observed that the extent of use of PEN Online can vary significantly over time and that the authorities of a number of registered importing countries do not actively use the system, and those countries thus remain vulnerable to the diversion of precursors. The authorities of a number of exporting countries have reported a lack of response on the part of the authorities of importing countries, even in cases in which a response was specifically requested. Likewise, authorities in an exporting country who give only a couple of days for the importing country's authorities to verify the legitimacy of a shipment or who send a pre-export notification after a shipment has been dispatched are not acting in line with established procedures. **INCB urges Governments that have not yet done so to register with the PEN Online system without further delay. INCB also**

urges all registered users of PEN Online to use the system actively and systematically and to notify the importing country of every planned shipment prior to dispatching it. Receiving authorities are also advised to follow up on the information available in order to ensure that there are no doubts about the legitimacy of the end use of shipments.

34. Some countries have exported significant amounts of precursors without pre-export notifications. For example, analysis of licit trade data provided by importing countries on form D and of data from PEN Online suggests that China and India both exported phenylacetic acid to Pakistan, a country that has invoked article 12, paragraph 10 (a), of the 1988 Convention in relation to that substance, without sending any pre-export notification via the PEN Online system. Similarly, Israel sent shipments of isosafrole without sending any pre-export notifications via the PEN Online system to several countries requiring such notifications. Also, Saudi Arabia continued to export precursor chemicals without sending any pre-export notifications via the PEN Online system. Shipments dispatched without pre-export notifications are at greater risk of being diverted, in particular if they are destined for countries that do not have in place a control system based on individual import permits. **INCB wishes to remind all Governments to use the PEN Online system for the notification of all planned exports of substances in Table I or II of the 1988 Convention, since that system represents the most efficient and effective way for the authorities of exporting and importing countries worldwide to communicate with each other.**

35. INCB also wishes to remind Governments that in order to ensure that they are informed of all planned shipments instantaneously, they must formally invoke the provisions of article 12, paragraph 10 (a), of the 1988 Convention and register with the PEN Online system. Either action alone is insufficient and does not automatically initiate the other. Currently, there are five countries and territories[12] that have invoked article 12, paragraph 10 (a), but are not using PEN Online, and there are 48 countries[13] that have registered to use PEN Online but have not yet invoked article 12, paragraph 10 (a) (see map 1).

---

[11] Angola, Antigua and Barbuda, Botswana, Cameroon, Central African Republic, Comoros, Democratic People's Republic of Korea, Democratic Republic of the Congo, Djibouti, Dominica, Equatorial Guinea, Fiji, Gabon, Gambia, Guinea, Guinea-Bissau, Guyana, Kiribati, Kuwait, Lesotho, Liberia, Malawi, Maldives, Mauritania, Monaco, Mongolia, Mozambique, Nauru, Niger, Palau, Papua New Guinea, Saint Kitts and Nevis, Samoa, San Marino, Sao Tome and Principe, Somalia, South Sudan, Swaziland, the former Yugoslav Republic of Macedonia, Timor-Leste, Togo, Tonga, Tunisia, Turkmenistan, Tuvalu and Vanuatu.

[12] Antigua and Barbuda, Cayman Islands, Maldives, Togo and Tonga.

[13] Albania, Andorra, Bahamas, Bahrain, Belize, Bhutan, Bosnia and Herzegovina, Brunei Darussalam, Burkina Faso, Burundi, Cabo Verde, Cambodia, Chad, Congo, Cuba, Eritrea, Georgia, Grenada, Guatemala, Honduras, Iceland, Iran (Islamic Republic of), Israel, Lao People's Democratic Republic, Mali, Marshall Islands, Mauritius, Micronesia (Federated States of), Montenegro, Morocco, Myanmar, Namibia, Nepal, New Zealand, Rwanda, Saint Lucia, Senegal, Serbia, Seychelles, Solomon Islands, Suriname, Uganda, Ukraine, Uruguay, Uzbekistan, Viet Nam, Yemen and Zambia.

Box 1

Minimum action for international trade monitoring through the Pre-Export Notification Online system

All countries that import and/or export substances in Tables I and II of the 1988 Convention should register with the PEN Online system by contacting INCB at pen@incb.org. Use of the system is free of charge. INCB should be notified immediately of any changes relating to PEN Online users.

All registered users should make active and systematic use of the PEN Online system for every transaction involving a substance in Table I or II of the Convention, both as sender and recipient of pre-export notifications.

Action by the authorities of importing countries:

- Invoke article 12, paragraph 10 (a), of the 1988 Convention

- Review all incoming pre-export notifications and comply with the deadlines for responses set by the exporting country's authorities, as necessary

- Where the authorities of an exporting country explicitly request a reply before authorizing a shipment, the authorities of importing countries should make every effort to respond to the pre-export notification to avoid delays and implications for legitimate trade

- Where more time is required by the authorities of an importing country to verify the legitimacy of a particular shipment, inform the exporting country's authorities through the PEN Online reply function and request the delivery to be delayed pending the outcome of the verification

Action by the authorities of exporting countries:

- Where the authorities of an importing country have formally requested to be notified of planned shipments of all or some substances in Table I of the 1988 Convention, it is a legal obligation under article 12 of the 1988 Convention to send pre-export notifications. Where an importing Government has requested the extension of the provisions of article 12, paragraph 10 (a), to all or some substances in Table II, it is advisable to provide notifications for shipments of those substances as well

- Authorities of exporting countries should send pre-export notifications in a systematic and comprehensive manner — in other words, notifications should be sent for all planned shipments to all importing countries whose authorities have formally requested to be informed and for all substances for which pre-export notifications have been requested. Pursuant to article 12, paragraph 10 (a), of the 1988 Convention, the pre-export notification should be sent before the shipment leaves for the importing country

- Where the authorities of exporting countries have a concern about the legitimacy of a shipment, they may consider authorizing the shipment only upon receiving an explicit response from the authorities of the importing country.

G. Activities and achievements in international precursor control

1. Project Prism and Project Cohesion

36. Two international initiatives led by INCB, Project Prism and Project Cohesion, continue to provide platforms for international cooperation in matters related to substances used in the illicit manufacture of amphetamine-type stimulants (the focus of Project Prism) and heroin and cocaine (the focus of Project Cohesion). Both projects are steered by the INCB Precursor Task Force and provide platforms for time-bound operations with a view to gathering information on potential gaps or weak links in international precursor control, on new trafficking trends, on modi operandi, on the actual use of the target chemicals in the illicit manufacture of drugs and on how those chemicals enter the clandestine laboratory environment. The projects are thus aimed at assisting Governments in ensuring the necessary level of alertness and developing specific risk profiles to prevent future diversions and — ultimately — to identify the trafficking organizations involved.

37. Communication among participants in the two projects is assisted — on an ongoing basis — by PICS (see paras. 45-47 below). Participants are also notified through special alerts about suspicious shipments and diversions and attempted diversions of precursors, as well as newly emerging precursors. In the reporting period, seven alerts were issued to inform Project Prism and Project Cohesion focal points about a number of non-scheduled chemicals found to have been used as pre-precursors or alternatives to scheduled substances in the illicit manufacture of drugs; the attempted importation of 10 tons of P-2-P into the Syrian

Arab Republic; the seizure of 2.9 tons of "chloro(pseudo)ephedrine"[14] in Germany; the domestic diversion of ephedrine in Nigeria after its importation; the final results of Operation Eagle Eye on the domestic movement and risk profiling of acetic anhydride trafficking; inconsistencies with regard to the availability of illicitly manufactured drugs in consumer markets and the reported levels of incidents involving the corresponding precursor chemicals; and the smuggling of pseudoephedrine tablets across Europe.

38. During the reporting period, the INCB Precursor Task Force conducted a global operation focusing on suspicious orders, shipments and thefts of methylamine (monomethylamine), a non-scheduled substance required in the illicit manufacture of a number of drugs, such as methamphetamine and 3,4-methylenedioxymethamphetamine (MDMA), the precursor ephedrine and several new psychoactive substances, especially those in the group called synthetic cathinones. A preliminary evaluation of the operation, known as Operation MMA, was conducted at the meeting of the Precursor Task Force held in Mexico City in June 2015. While — with few exceptions — no suspicious activities were identified during Operation MMA, the operation resulted in improved knowledge of the number and type of operators involved in the manufacture of, trade in and distribution of methylamine and provided valuable practical information on how to approach non-scheduled chemicals. A total of 39 countries and territories participated in Operation MMA.

39. The INCB Precursor Task Force also discussed the current status of information on precursors that continue to feed the illicit processing of cocaine and heroin, and noted that there continued to be little or no information about the sources of those precursors, which are listed in Tables I and II of the 1988 Convention, or their substitutes.

40. Participants in the Group of Experts on Chemical Substances and Pharmaceutical Products of the Inter-American Drug Abuse Control Commission (CICAD) were surveyed to help improve knowledge of the suspected sources of potassium permanganate, the modi operandi used for its domestic diversion and the adequacy of control measures applied to acids and solvents in Table II of the 1988 Convention. Preliminary results confirm the value of and the need to enhance: (a) measures to prevent diversion of those chemicals from domestic distribution channels; and (b) cooperation with industry. The participants also confirmed the need for consistent and comprehensive implementation of the PEN Online system. The results of the survey will be discussed at the next meeting of the Precursor Task Force, to be held in 2016.

41. In order for the successful continuation of international activities under Project Prism and Project Cohesion, up-to-date contact details of national focal points are critical for ensuring rapid and direct communication between the authorities concerned. **INCB therefore encourages all Governments to review the contact lists available on its secure website and ensure that the details of their Project Prism and Cohesion focal points are up to date. INCB also encourages active participation in operations conducted under Project Prism and Project Cohesion and follow-up on the action identified.**

Box 2

Minimum action for international cooperation under Project Prism and Project Cohesion

The authorities of all countries and territories should endeavour to nominate a focal point (or central national authority or designated authority) for Project Prism and/or Project Cohesion.

Existing contact details of focal points on the secure website of INCB should be reviewed to ensure that all information is correct and up to date; the Board should be notified immediately of any changes.

The focal point should be given the necessary authority to function as the sole entity in the country responsible for communicating with all other countries regarding Project Prism and/or Project Cohesion and should:

- Receive and process (or facilitate the processing of) information about licit precursor transactions and suspicious or illicit incidents involving precursors

- Actively gather and communicate information related to the national precursor situation and trends (using PICS where possible or applicable)

- Respond to requests from other focal points, INCB and other international organizations concerned regarding precursor-related matters and make available relevant data and documentation to support international investigations

- Ensure active participation of his or her country in relevant time-bound operations under Project Prism and Project Cohesion and, to that end, ensure coordination at the national level

---

14 The term "chloro(pseudo)ephedrine" is used to reflect the fact that the substance is typically a mixture of the diastereoisomeric forms of what are commonly known as chloroephedrine and chloropseudoephedrine.

2. Other international initiatives focusing on precursor control

42.   A regional operation was conducted in October 2014 with the participation of the competent national authorities of Afghanistan, Iran (Islamic Republic of), Kazakhstan, Kyrgyzstan, Pakistan, Tajikistan, Turkmenistan and Uzbekistan to identify and intercept smuggled shipments of acetic anhydride and certain non-scheduled chemicals suspected of being used in illicit heroin processing or of being used as a "cover load" for (i.e. to conceal) acetic anhydride. The results of the operation are currently being analysed and subsequent phases are being planned.

43.   China, the Lao People's Democratic Republic, Myanmar and Thailand continued to formalize their cooperation in the context of "Safe Mekong", a joint operation aimed at addressing illicit drug production and distribution in the area of the upper Mekong and the Golden Triangle. During the second phase of the operation, in early 2015, more than 30 tons of unspecified chemicals were seized, along with various drugs and cutting agents, and a significant number of drug traffickers were arrested. Consideration is being given to the possibility of including Cambodia and Viet Nam in the operation.

44.   INCB, in cooperation with the United Nations Office on Drugs and Crime (UNODC), organized an international conference entitled Precursor Chemicals and New Psychoactive Substances in Bangkok from 21 to 24 April 2015. The conference brought together some 200 participants from 37 countries and regional and international organizations to discuss the latest challenges relating to precursor control and new psychoactive substances, as well as approaches to collectively address those challenges at the global and regional levels. As a contribution to the special session of the General Assembly to be held in 2016, the conference adopted an outcome document on proposed measures against the misuse of scheduled and non-scheduled precursors and new psychoactive substances.

3. Precursors Incident Communication System

45.   In March 2012, INCB launched PICS as a communication platform to allow relevant government authorities to share and acquire information, in real time, about individual precursor incidents (including seizures, shipments stopped in transit and illicit laboratories), with a view to alerting each other about emerging trends in precursor trafficking and the modi operandi of the

diversion of precursors and facilitating the launching of joint investigations.

46.   As at 1 November 2015, the PICS user base had grown to more than 480 users, representing some 200 agencies in 94 countries and territories and 10 regional and international agencies (see map 2). Registration with PICS is cost-free, and PICS is easy for government authorities to access and use. The PICS online tool is now available in four languages: English, French, Russian and Spanish. Utilization of the PICS communication platform remains an essential measure for Governments to take as part of their efforts to ensure comprehensive precursor control. **INCB commends all Governments using PICS and encourages those Governments that have not yet registered as PICS users to nominate focal points for each of their relevant national authorities involved in precursor control, such as regulatory, law enforcement and specialized drug control agencies.**

47.   Since the launch of PICS, more than 1,350 incidents, involving 84 different countries and territories, have been communicated. Incidents involving chemicals not under international control, including substances on the limited international special surveillance list of non-scheduled chemicals, as well as other non-scheduled chemicals, account for an increasing proportion of all incidents communicated via PICS and underline the value of PICS in helping to identify emerging trends. **INCB commends the sharing of information about individual precursor incidents, especially if the information is shared early, because it alerts authorities in other countries to relevant trafficking cases, modi operandi and emerging developments involving precursors, thus helping them to detect similar incidents in those countries, build up cases and be better prepared to address new trends.**[15]

---

[15] Governments that have not yet registered their PICS focal points may request an account at pics@incb.org.

Box 3

Minimum action for sharing information about precursor incidents through the Precursors Incident Communication System

The authorities of all countries and territories should endeavour to nominate users for PICS. The users should include personnel from the widest possible range of national authorities concerned with precursor issues, who effect seizures, investigate diversions or attempted diversions of precursor chemicals, or who might otherwise be in a position to identify, suspend or stop suspicious shipments entering, transiting or leaving their territory. The users should therefore not be limited to focal points from regulatory authorities or central law enforcement agencies but should include staff from all the law enforcement agencies concerned (police, customs, military etc.) at all levels, such as those that need to communicate precursor incidents with, or receive information on seizures of precursors from, agencies worldwide.

Registered PICS users should communicate incidents in real time to alert other PICS users as early as possible about incidents, modi operandi and new trends and enable them to quickly cooperate or follow up at their

end. To the extent possible, users should avoid situations in which seizures are reported on the official website of the seizing authorities and not communicated through PICS at the same time.

Registered users should actively use PICS and communicate actionable information on precursor incidents, including incidents involving non-scheduled chemicals, and, where available, routing information (source, transit, destination), company information and any pictures of labels and relevant documentation.

Registered users from a country named in the incident as either the source country, a transit country or the country of destination should contact the incident owner in the country where the incident occurred to obtain further details on the nature and extent of his or her country's involvement and to exchange documents for the initiation or further pursuit of an investigation.

After the conclusion of an investigation, the information on the PICS incident concerned should be updated.

Map 2. Governments that have registered with and used the Precursors Incident Communication System (as at 1 November 2015)

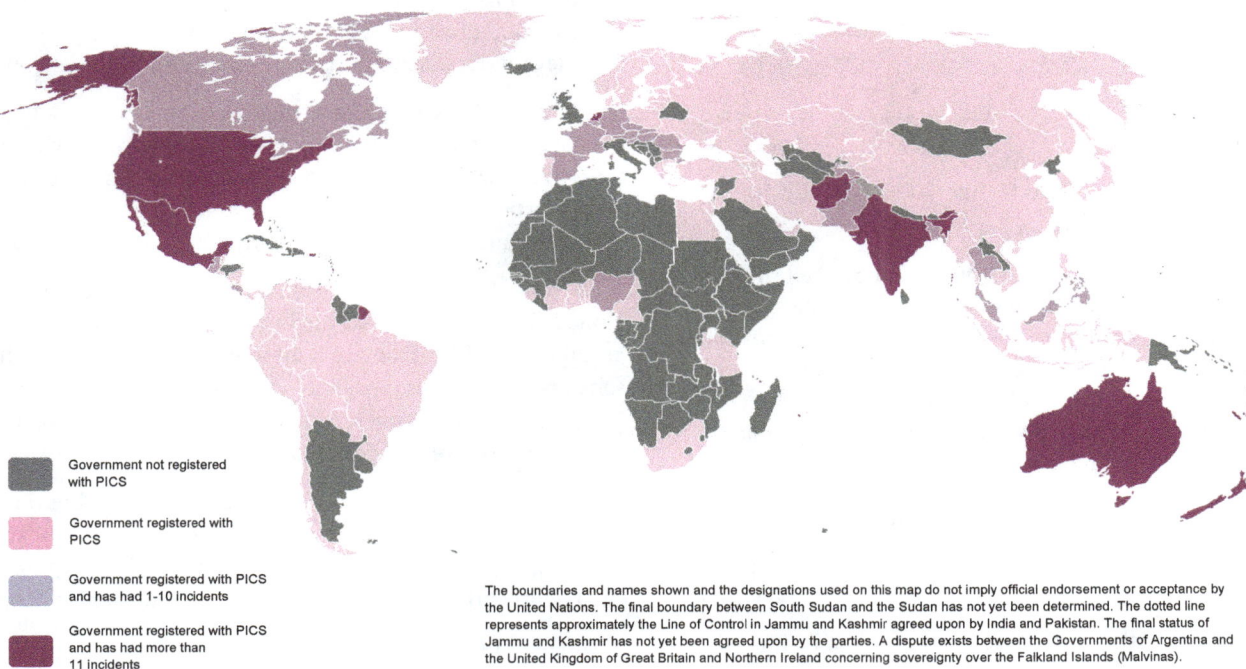

Government not registered with PICS

Government registered with PICS

Government registered with PICS and has had 1-10 incidents

Government registered with PICS and has had more than 11 incidents

The boundaries and names shown and the designations used on this map do not imply official endorsement or acceptance by the United Nations. The final boundary between South Sudan and the Sudan has not yet been determined. The dotted line represents approximately the Line of Control in Jammu and Kashmir agreed upon by India and Pakistan. The final status of Jammu and Kashmir has not yet been agreed upon by the parties. A dispute exists between the Governments of Argentina and the United Kingdom of Great Britain and Northern Ireland concerning sovereignty over the Falkland Islands (Malvinas).

III. Extent of licit trade in precursors and the latest trends in precursor trafficking

48.   The present chapter provides an overview of major trends and developments in both licit trade and trafficking in precursor chemicals for the period 1 November 2014 to 1 November 2015. It contains a summary of information on seizures and cases of diversion, attempted diversion and suspended or stopped shipments in international trade and, where known, domestic distribution channels, as well as activities associated with illicit drug manufacture. The analysis draws on information submitted to INCB through various mechanisms, such as PEN Online, form D (for 2014), Project Prism and Project Cohesion, as well as through PICS and direct notifications from Governments.

49.   INCB wishes to thank all Governments for the information received. Readers are reminded that the data must be seen in the context of significant year-on-year variations in reported seizure data that occur as a result of inconsistent reporting by Governments and in the light of the fact that seizures of precursors, more than seizures of drugs, generally reflect the results of large individual seizures and targeted regulatory and law enforcement initiatives. In addition, seizures of precursors are often the result of cooperation among several countries, and therefore the occurrence and magnitude of seizures made in a given country should not be misinterpreted or overestimated in assessing that country's role in the overall precursor trafficking situation.

A. Substances used in the illicit manufacture of amphetamine-type stimulants

1. Substances used in the illicit manufacture of amphetamines

50.   Many of the precursors that could be used in the illicit manufacture of amphetamines (i.e. amphetamine and methamphetamine) are widely traded internationally. During the reporting period, the authorities of 38 exporting countries used the PEN Online system for almost 5,800 transactions involving shipments of precursors of amphetamine and methamphetamine.

(a) Ephedrine and pseudoephedrine

Licit trade

51.   During the reporting period, 5,260 transactions involving ephedrine and pseudoephedrine were recorded

through the PEN Online system. The notifications were for shipments totalling more than 2,300 tons of pseudoephedrine and 114 tons of ephedrine. The shipments of ephedrine and pseudoephedrine originated in 35 exporting countries and territories and were destined for 154 importing countries and territories.

52.   As noted in the Board's 2014 report on precursors,[16] traffickers are still trying to use licit channels of international trade as sources of ephedrine and pseudoephedrine, albeit significantly less than they did before 2010. On form D for 2014, Luxembourg reported having stopped a shipment of 500 kg of ephedrine to Ghana, and Latvia reported having stopped a shipment of 300 kg of pseudoephedrine preparations to Belarus. In both cases, additional information was not provided, such as information on whether or not the shipments were stopped in transit or at their initial point of export or information on the modi operandi of the traffickers. The suspension of shipments by exporting countries also occurred, on a more regular basis, as a result of the authorities of importing countries objecting through the PEN Online system to planned shipments.

53.   Malaysia reported on form D a case involving the theft of 5 kg of pseudoephedrine preparations from the warehouse of the manufacturer. In 2015, INCB was informed of three additional cases involving the theft of pseudoephedrine:

    (a)   In the first case, 150 kg of pseudoephedrine — the contents of 6 drums in a group of 48 drums — disappeared from a shipment of the substance totalling 1.2 tons en route from India to Switzerland while transiting the port of Antwerp, Belgium. Indian authorities provided the relevant documentation. An investigation is under way;

    (b)   The second case involved the loss of 400 kg from a total of 5 tons of pseudoephedrine hydrochloride en route from India to the United Kingdom of Great Britain and Northern Ireland via Sri Lanka. The authorities concerned are cooperating in the investigation of the case;

    (c)   In the third instance, the authorities of the United Kingdom reported the loss or theft of about 5 kg of pseudoephedrine from a shipment to Uganda. The substance had disappeared during shipping from a 25-kilogram drum; someone had tampered with the seal of the drum. An investigation is taking place.

54.   INCB has previously expressed concern about the diversion and attempted diversion of ephedrine and pseudoephedrine in and from Pakistan that had begun to emerge in 2010. Attempts to divert the substances from

---

16 E/INCB/2014/4, para. 86.

legitimate international trade have, since mid-2012, led to several individuals being prosecuted in an ongoing case that involves the allocation of ephedrine to pharmaceutical companies for the manufacture of pharmaceutical preparations in amounts exceeding the quotas established in national regulations.[17]

55. Similar major court cases are taking place elsewhere. In 2015, there were ongoing investigations in Argentina of major diversion cases dating back to 2008, when that country was identified as one of the main sources of raw ephedrine and pseudoephedrine diverted to supply illicit methamphetamine manufacture in Mexico,[18] where the import of those substances was banned in 2008. Argentine authorities have since introduced stricter controls on the importation and end use of ephedrines, including in the form of pharmaceutical preparations.

Trafficking

56. A total of 27 countries reported on form D for 2014 seizures of ephedrine (either as raw material or in the form of pharmaceutical preparations) totalling nearly 33 tons. The bulk of the seizures of ephedrine as raw material were reported by China (31.5 tons), followed by the Philippines (510 kg) and Australia (460 kg). China also accounted for nearly the entire amount of reported seizures of ephedrine in the form of pharmaceutical preparations (3.2 tons); all the other countries together accounted for just over 40 kg of the seizures of ephedrine in the form of pharmaceutical preparations. A total of 16 countries reported on form D for 2014 seizures of pseudoephedrine, including 350 kg of pseudoephedrine as raw material and 1.3 tons of pseudoephedrine in the form of pharmaceutical preparations. Seizures of pseudoephedrine preparations amounting to more than 100 kg were reported by Bulgaria (840 kg), the Czech Republic (350 kg) and Malaysia (112 kg).

57. The seizures of pseudoephedrine in Bulgaria and the Czech Republic in 2015 were largely related to a development observed since 2012 involving the smuggling of pseudoephedrine tablets across Europe. The tablets usually originated in Turkey and were destined for Poland; they had a relatively high pseudoephedrine content, up to 120 mg per tablet, and typically also contained an antihistamine. Increasingly aware of the phenomenon, Turkish authorities intensified their inspections of pharmacies, fined those that had sold the preparation without a prescription and in wholesale quantities and tried them in court for engaging in organized criminal activity.

While the investigations are ongoing, Turkish regulatory authorities have classified the product concerned as a controlled preparation requiring import and export authorization (see para. 18 above).

58. Malaysia also reported significant seizures of ephedrine and pseudoephedrine, including the seizure of 287 kg of pseudoephedrine raw material originating in India and the seizure in an illicit methamphetamine laboratory of 112 kg of pseudoephedrine in the form of pharmaceutical preparations of unknown origin; 33 kg of ephedrine preparations were also seized in an illicit laboratory.

59. The Philippines reported the seizure of 510 kg of ephedrine raw material of unknown origin and the dismantling of two large-scale illicit methamphetamine laboratories, estimated to be capable of producing between 15 and 100 kg of methamphetamine hydrochloride each day. In September 2014, Philippine authorities also seized in two warehouses more than 650 kg of 1,2-dimethyl-3-phenylaziridine, a non-scheduled intermediate in the manufacture of methamphetamine using ephedrine. As that represented the first notification of 1,2-dimethyl-3-phenylaziridine to INCB, and as the substance is also known as an artefact from laboratory analysis of "chloro(pseudo)ephedrine", the Board enquired with the relevant authorities. The reply is still pending. In connection with the evidence uncovered in the two warehouses, the authorities noted the possibility of a shift in the ephedrine-based manufacturing method used, from the traditional Nagai method (using red phosphorus) to the so-called Birch method (using lithium metal and ammonia), and the related reduction in manufacturing costs.

60. Australia reported on form D for 2014 a total of 215 seizures of ephedrine raw material, amounting to nearly 460 kg and originating in China (266 kg), China, Hong Kong Special Administrative Region (116 kg), Malaysia (30 kg), the United States of America (7 kg) and Viet Nam (38 kg). Other significant seizures of ephedrine originated in Lebanon (66 kg, concealed in jars of tomato paste) and India (37 kg, concealed in henna powder).[19] A small amount (10 kg) of pseudoephedrine raw material was seized in Australia in 2014. For the second consecutive year, there have not been any reports in Australia about seizures of pseudoephedrine preparations in the form of ContacNT, a product that used to originate in China; since 2012, authorities in China have gradually tightened controls over ContacNT.

---

[17] E/INCB/2012/4, para. 22.
[18] E/INCB/2009/4, para. 57.

[19] Australian Crime Commission, *Illicit Drug Data Report 2013-2014.*

61. Through PICS, Australia also communicated the seizure of a number of shipments in international freight and the mailing system involving amounts of up to 20 kg of pseudoephedrine hidden in loose tea leaves from the Islamic Republic of Iran. A shipment from Iraq of 1.3 tons of tea leaves containing up to 90 kg of pseudoephedrine was also intercepted in Australia. Pakistan reported on form D for 2014 seizures of ephedrine with a gross weight of some 35 kg; the ephedrine had been concealed in tea leaves.

62. The trend observed in Australia involving a shift from seizures of pseudoephedrine in the form of pharmaceutical preparations to ephedrine also appears to be emerging in New Zealand. Authorities in New Zealand have reported a significant increase in seizures of ephedrine on the border, whereas previously such seizures had mostly been seizures of pseudoephedrine in the form of pharmaceutical preparations, principally ContacNT. At the same time, ephedrine has so far been seized from only a few of the usually small-scale illicit laboratories feeding the methamphetamine market in New Zealand. Authorities suspect that the change in preference of precursor is linked with changes in the size and sophistication of illicit laboratories dismantled in the country. Nevertheless, the costs of obtaining the required precursors and then manufacturing methamphetamine in New Zealand continued to be significantly higher than those for obtaining the same amount of end product abroad.

63. Chinese authorities uncovered one of the biggest manufacturing cases in 2014, which resulted in the seizure of 1.6 tons of ephedrine and 1 ton of methcathinone, a substance in Schedule I of the Convention on Psychotropic Substances of 1971[20] that is an intermediate in the manufacture of ephedrine from 2-bromopropiophenone. In August 2014, a case involving the smuggling of a precursor chemical to New Zealand was uncovered by Chinese authorities in Fujian Province, resulting in five arrests and the seizure of 46 kg of ephedrine in China and subsequently a number of arrests and seizures of ephedrine totalling about 200 kg in New Zealand.[21]

64. Forensic profiling of samples of methamphetamine seized by Japanese customs authorities supports earlier findings suggesting regional differences in the starting materials and synthesis methods used for illicit methamphetamine manufacture. The samples of methamphetamine originating in Asia and Africa appeared to have been manufactured using as starting material ephedrine or pseudoephedrine and as reagents either thionyl chloride (i.e. employing the Emde method) or

hydriodic acid and red phosphorus (i.e. employing the Nagai method). It was found that methamphetamine routed into Japan from Mexico was typically made using P-2-P-based methods. More than 95 per cent of the samples were found to contain the more potent d-methamphetamine.

65. Clandestine laboratories manufacturing methamphetamine from ephedrine or pseudoephedrine were reported by the Governments of a few countries. Indonesian authorities seized a small-scale clandestine laboratory in which methamphetamine was being manufactured from ephedrine; other seized precursor chemicals included acetone, hydrochloric acid and toluene, all of which had been obtained from sources within Indonesia.

66. In Nigeria, three laboratories illicitly manufacturing methamphetamine were dismantled in May 2015, bringing to 10 the total number of such laboratories dismantled in that country since 2011. In addition, Nigerian authorities have discovered what appear to be the sites of a number of recently evacuated methamphetamine laboratories, suggesting that traffickers have been operating a chain of laboratories that are moved in order to avoid detection. The trend noted in 2013 whereby the sites of laboratories shifted to more remote areas continued: all the laboratories identified up to May 2015 were located in Anambra State, in south-eastern Nigeria. Available information suggests that the same method of methamphetamine synthesis was employed in all the laboratories, using ephedrine, hypophosphorous acid and iodine; crystallization of methamphetamine hydrochloride was performed using acetone or toluene.

67. In most of the methamphetamine laboratories seized in Nigeria, only traces of the key precursor, ephedrine, were found and the sources of the chemicals were generally not known. However, there is now increasing evidence that precursors are being obtained locally, from domestic distribution channels, after they have been legally imported. Several incidents involving domestic diversions of ephedrine are being investigated. Chief officials of the companies concerned were often involved in the diversions, and it is suspected that the diverted substances were used to illicitly manufacture methamphetamine in laboratories not only in Nigeria but also outside the country.

68. Nigerian authorities have stepped up their efforts to monitor imports of precursor chemicals and the use of the imported chemicals by companies that are the end users. The incidents in Nigeria serve as a reminder that diversion can and does happen at all stages of the distribution chain. **INCB wishes to encourage all competent national authorities to remain vigilant not only regarding the**

---

20 United Nations, *Treaty Series*, vol. 1019, No. 14956.

21 National Narcotics Control Commission of China, *Annual Report on Drug Control in China 2015* (Beijing, 2015).

diversion of precursor chemicals from international trade but also regarding their diversion from domestic distribution channels and to pay particular attention to the legitimate final use of key precursor chemicals and the quantity required for that purpose.

69. South Africa remains a key destination for smuggled ephedrine and pseudoephedrine. One of the largest shipments of smuggled ephedrine or pseudoephedrine destined for South Africa — 83 kg of ephedrine — was seized in Nigeria in February 2015. In addition, a number of incidents involving passengers smuggling ephedrine or pseudoephedrine occurred at the international airport at New Delhi; the passengers' intended destination was South Africa. Authorities in Zimbabwe reported seizures of 70 kg of ephedrine in four incidents at Harare International Airport; in all four incidents, South African nationals acted as couriers and Zimbabwe was the intended destination.

70. African countries have occasionally reported on form D seizures of ephedrine or pseudoephedrine that were linked to the abuse of those substances for their stimulant properties and not linked to the use of those substances as precursors in illicit methamphetamine manufacture. Unsubstantiated high estimates of annual legitimate requirements and imports, as well as smuggling, feed that illicit market. Monitoring is further complicated by the fact that in many cases ephedrine and pseudoephedrine are abused in the form of pharmaceutical preparations containing those substances, and pre-export notifications of shipments of such preparations are often not systematically issued through the PEN Online system.

71. The situation with regard to trafficking in ephedrine and pseudoephedrine in some parts of West Asia remains unclear. Several countries in the region report significant seizures of amphetamine-type stimulants, mainly amphetamine (in the form of Captagon) and methamphetamine; however, the sites used for illicitly manufacturing the drugs and the sources of the precursors used remain largely unknown, as few countries in the region provide seizure information on form D. Political instability in a number of countries in West Asia adds to the difficulties encountered in national and international precursor control efforts. Nevertheless, this situation, which INCB drew attention to in its 2014 report on precursors,[22] remains a matter of serious concern. **In the light of the prevailing situation in several countries in West Asia, such as the Syrian Arab Republic, INCB encourages all countries to exercise a heightened level of vigilance regarding large-scale orders for pseudoephedrine placed by companies in conflict areas and to consider suspending the authorization of such**

shipments unless there is explicit confirmation regarding the legitimacy of the shipment and the end use of the substance, and secure transportation and handling can be assured.

72. In the Islamic Republic of Iran, methamphetamine supply indicators declined in 2014, as Iranian authorities dismantled 340 small-scale laboratories (a decrease of 24 per cent compared with the 2013 figure) and seized 2.6 tons of crystalline methamphetamine (a decrease of 28 per cent compared with the 2013 figure). Iranian authorities cited the special situation in northern Iraq as a reason for ephedrine being smuggled into Iranian territory, as well as the significant profits resulting from smuggling illicitly manufactured methamphetamine into South-East Asia.[23]

73. Increasing concerns about methamphetamine trafficking, abuse and manufacture in Afghanistan have also led authorities there to assess the adequacy of domestic procedures related to the import and distribution of pharmaceutical preparations containing ephedrine and pseudoephedrine. Preliminary results indicate that most shipments of such preparations were not properly declared at customs offices and were not registered by the competent authority for distribution in the country.

74. With the tightening of precursor control legislation in South America and in Central America and the Caribbean, the number and size of reported seizures of precursor chemicals have decreased. In 2014, of all the countries in those regions, only Argentina reported seizures of ephedrine (24 kg) on form D. **While these successes are commendable, INCB wishes to remind all Governments of the importance of implementing existing regulations systematically and consistently and encourages Governments to remain vigilant regarding changes in the modi operandi of traffickers of precursors and the possibility of a country being targeted once again by traffickers.**

75. The almost complete absence of reports of seizures of ephedrine and pseudoephedrine is also evident in North America: United States authorities reported on form D for 2014 the seizure of a total of only 20 kg of ephedrine and pseudoephedrine in all their forms. This contrasts sharply with the situation just a few years earlier, when the United States reported having seized a number of tons of ephedrine and pseudoephedrine. Nevertheless, in the United States small-scale laboratories illicitly manufacturing methamphetamine have continued to use as starting material ephedrines in the form of pharmaceutical preparations obtained through an activity known as

---

22 E/INCB/2014/4, para. 61.

23 Islamic Republic of Iran, Drug Control Headquarters, *Drug Control in 2014* (Niktasvir Publishing, March 2015), pp. 53 and 60.

"smurfing", which involves making a series of purchases from multiple retail distributors to circumvent established purchase limits. United States authorities estimate that domestic methamphetamine manufacture has decreased, most likely as a result of the increased availability of methamphetamine illicitly manufactured in Mexico. Another new trend is the smuggling of liquid methamphetamine into the United States for subsequent recrystallization or recovery in that country; the process is not complicated but it requires a significant amount of solvents such as acetone.

76. Mexico did not report any seizures of ephedrine or pseudoephedrine, confirming the predominant use of P-2-P-based methods in illicit methamphetamine manufacture in that country.

77. Information from India, communicated through PICS, confirmed that in that country seizures continued to be made of ephedrine and pseudoephedrine in the form of raw material and pharmaceutical preparations. The individual seizures were in amounts of up to 25 kg, with few exceptions, such as two cases of domestic diversion of 250 kg and 100 kg of pseudoephedrine in August 2015. During the first eight months of 2015, India did not detect any facilities illicitly manufacturing amphetamine-type stimulants. Information about the dismantling of an alleged illicit ephedrine manufacturing unit is being verified.

(b) Norephedrine and ephedra

Licit trade

78. Analysis of international trade data reported through the PEN Online system revealed that between 1 November 2014 and 1 November 2015 12 countries exported norephedrine to 30 countries and that the shipments involved a total of almost 20.5 tons of the substance. Although it is increasing, international trade in norephedrine, a substance that can be used in the illicit manufacture of amphetamine, remains at a low level compared with trade in other precursors.

Trafficking

79. Seizures of norephedrine were reported on form D for 2014 by only three countries (Australia, China and Philippines), in amounts of less than 100 grams.

80. For the third consecutive year, no seizures of ephedra were reported on form D. China continued to seize ephedra in 2014, according to information in the annual report on drug control in that country. However, seizures of ephedra amounted to only 423 tons, a significant decrease compared with the 2013 figure; Chinese authorities attribute that decrease to the implementation of strengthened controls in

ephedra-producing areas of the Inner Mongolia Autonomous Region, the Xinjiang Uighur Autonomous Region, Gansu Province and the Ningxia Autonomous Region of China.[24] **INCB wishes to remind Governments to remain vigilant regarding the possibility of ephedra, a natural source of ephedrine, or ephedra-based products being illicitly used on their territory.**

(c) 1-Phenyl-2-propanone, phenylacetic acid and *alpha*-phenylacetoacetonitrile

81. P-2-P is an immediate precursor in the illicit manufacture of amphetamine and methamphetamine with very few legitimate uses other than the manufacture of those substances for pharmaceutical purposes. P-2-P can be synthesized from phenylacetic acid and APAAN. Non-scheduled esters of phenylacetic acid and other pre-precursors may be used as substitutes for P-2-P in the illicit manufacture of amphetamine and methamphetamine (see paras. 104, 105 and 115 below and annex IV).

Licit trade

82. International trade in P-2-P is limited, in terms of both the volume and the number of countries involved: during the reporting period, six exporting countries sent, via the PEN Online system, to 10 importing countries pre-export notifications for the planned exportation of 25 shipments of P-2-P, amounting to almost 33,000 litres. By contrast, licit trade in phenylacetic acid, an immediate precursor of P-2-P, is far more significant in terms of both the number of countries involved and the total amount traded: during the reporting period, 13 exporting countries sent pre-export notifications to 50 importing countries about 458 planned shipments of phenylacetic acid, amounting to 254 tons. There was only one transaction involving APAAN.

83. Investigations into an attempted import of more than 9,000 litres of P-2-P into the Syrian Arab Republic by a previously unknown company continued. The shipment was stopped by the Indian authorities in response to a request made by the competent national authorities of the Syrian Arab Republic through PEN Online. Despite subsequent claims by other Syrian authorities that the shipment was legitimate, no delivery has been made from India. The Syrian Arab Republic has not submitted any annual legitimate requirements for P-2-P and the final end use could not be sufficiently substantiated. **INCB therefore recommends all exporting countries not to authorize any shipment of P-2-P to the Syrian Arab Republic unless its legitimate final use has been duly confirmed**

---

[24] National Narcotics Control Commission of China, *Annual Report on Drug Control in China 2015* (Beijing, 2015).

by the relevant competent national authorities. INCB requests all exporting countries to communicate to it any significant order placed for P-2-P to be exported to the Syrian Arab Republic or any other country in order to allow for follow-up with the competent national authorities.

Trafficking

84. Seizures of P-2-P were reported by 13 countries on form D for 2014; seizures of P-2-P in amounts in excess of 1,000 litres were reported by Mexico (5,900 litres), Myanmar (4,800 litres), China (3,200 litres) and Poland (1,400 litres). Lithuania and the Netherlands reported seizures of P-2-P in amounts of 400 to 700 litres, while other countries reported seizures of the substance in amounts not exceeding 50 litres. With the exception of the seizures of P-2-P reported by Myanmar and seizures of that substance in Australia and Ireland, which were reported to have originated in China, the seized P-2-P was typically of illicit origin; that is, the substance was seized in illicit laboratories and had been illicitly manufactured from pre-precursors such as APAAN or phenylacetic acid esters. Such incidents also continued in 2015 and were typically communicated by the Netherlands through PICS. This distinction is important because a case involving a precursor chemical diverted from legitimate sources requires an intervention that is very different from what is required in a case involving a precursor chemical illicitly manufactured from a scheduled or non-scheduled pre-precursor. INCB commends those Governments that have provided information about the origin of seized chemicals (i.e. whether they are of licit or illicit origin) and the country of origin, where applicable, and encourages all others to do the same in order to support the design of appropriate interventions worldwide.

85. INCB was informed about a seizure of almost 7,000 litres of P-2-P in Poland in March 2015. The substance was seized in a warehouse in the seaport of Gdansk, Poland, and was part of a shipment from China in 2012 containing a total of 32 tons of unspecified chemicals. The authorities concerned are cooperating in the investigation of the case.

86. Four countries reported on form D for 2014 seizures of phenylacetic acid, and seven countries reported seizures of APAAN.[25] The seizures of phenylacetic acid included large amounts seized in China (nearly 50 tons) and Mexico (more than 1.3 tons). The seizures in Mexico were associated with the illicit manufacture of P-2-P, most often from phenylacetic acid esters that are under national

control in Mexico but not under international control (see paras. 105 and 106 below). Estonia reported the seizure of 100 kg of phenylacetic acid in one instance but did not provide any information on the origin of the precursor chemical. In 2015, seizures of phenylacetic acid were also communicated through PICS; they typically occurred in illicit laboratories, often in the Netherlands.

87. APAAN seizures in 2014 amounted to more than 11 tons and were all reported by countries in Europe. This represents a significant decline compared with 2013, when a record amount of more than 43.5 tons of APAAN was seized. The largest amounts of APAAN were seized in 2014 in Germany; those seizures totalled more than 5.1 tons and included a shipment of 5 tons of the substance, en route to Poland, that was reported to have originated in China in February 2014, three months before the ban on the substance in China went into effect. The Netherlands reported seizing more than 3 tons of APAAN in eight instances, and Bulgaria reported seizing two shipments totalling nearly 2 tons that had entered the country by land from Turkey; Belgium, Poland and Romania reported seizures of APAAN in amounts of 100 to 600 kg. In the majority of those instances, information about the origin of the substance was not provided. In the first 10 months of 2015, seven incidents involving over 700 kg of APAAN were communicated through PICS; all but one incident occurred in the Netherlands.

88. Information about the substances used in the illicit manufacture of drugs can also be obtained from the forensic analysis of the drug end product. Relevant programmes have existed for many years for methamphetamine and have helped to confirm a shift from the use of ephedrines to P-2-P-based manufacturing methods for the illicit manufacture of that drug in North America. This trend peaked in mid-2014, when it was shown that more than 95 per cent of the analysed methamphetamine samples had been manufactured using P-2-P-based methods. More recently, the figure has dropped to 78 per cent and forensic profiling data suggest a shift to the use of benzaldehyde and nitroethane as alternative chemicals for the manufacture of P-2-P and subsequently methamphetamine. Mexico added these two chemicals to the list of controlled substances on 1 October 2015 (see para. 16 above).

89. By contrast, P-2-P has traditionally been the chemical of choice for illicit amphetamine manufacture in Europe. In this situation, forensic analysis can provide valuable information about the synthetic route and about whether a seized sample of P-2-P was diverted from legitimate sources or illicitly manufactured from APAAN, phenylacetic acid or its esters.

---

25 APAAN was included in Table I of the 1988 Convention effective 6 October 2014.

90. In Australia, a forensic drug-profiling programme analysing samples of methamphetamine seized at the border found that methamphetamine continued to be manufactured primarily from ephedrine and pseudoephedrine. However, starting in 2013 there was a slight increase in the proportion of the samples of seized methamphetamine that had been synthesized from P-2-P. This trend was also seen in relation to clandestine methamphetamine laboratories operating in Australia. **INCB encourages Governments that have the technical capabilities to conduct such detailed forensic analyses and offer such support, to the extent possible, to other Governments on request, with a view to improving knowledge of the chemicals actually being used in illicit drug manufacture and the sources of those chemicals, thus supporting precursor control measures worldwide.**

2. Substances used in the illicit manufacture of 3,4-methylenedioxymethamphetamine and its analogues

91. Four substances included in Table I of the 1988 Convention are precursors of "ecstasy"-type substances. 3,4-MDP-2-P is an immediate precursor of MDMA and other "ecstasy"-type substances, and it can be manufactured from piperonal, safrole or isosafrole (see annex IV). Licit trade in all those precursor chemicals except piperonal involves only a few countries, there have not been any significant diversions from international trade recently, and seizures of those chemicals vary from one year to another. However, several non-scheduled derivatives of 3,4-MDP-2-P are increasingly becoming available (see paras. 116-119 below) and may to some extent be contributing to the apparent increase in the availability of MDMA.

(a) 3,4-Methylenedioxyphenyl-2-propanone and piperonal

Licit trade

92. There is almost no legitimate industrial use for 3,4-MDP-2-P, and international trade in the substance is nearly non-existent; the opposite is true for piperonal. For 3,4-MDP-2-P, there was one pre-export notification for 3 litres sent through the PEN Online system, and only four Governments have a legitimate annual requirement for the import of more than 1 litre of the substance per year (see annex II). For piperonal, during the reporting period, 17 exporting countries used the PEN Online system to send pre-export notifications for 590 shipments of that substance, totalling almost 2,000 tons, to 51 importing countries.

Trafficking

93. Three countries (Australia, Belgium and China) reported seizures of 3,4-MDP-2-P on form D for 2014, and four countries (Australia, Estonia, Netherlands and Philippines) reported seizures of piperonal. The reported total amounts of less than 60 litres of 3,4-MDP-2-P and 5 litres of piperonal are negligible in comparison with the figures for the previous year; thus, the situation is similar to the situation in the period 2010-2011.

94. Through PICS, INCB was made aware of a seizure of 60 kg of 3,4-MDP-2-P in Australia in May 2015; the origin of the substance was China. Acting on information provided by Belgian customs authorities, authorities in China, Hong Kong Special Administrative Region, seized 1.5 tons of a substance identified as 3,4-MDP-2-P that had been stored at a warehouse pending exportation to Poland via Belgium. The source of the substance was allegedly in China but no additional documentation was available on site to confirm the alleged source. Investigations are still taking place.

95. During the reporting period, the authorities of the Netherlands communicated three seizures of piperonal through PICS. The seizures occurred in warehouses where precursors of various drugs were stored. Spanish authorities reported on form D that shipments containing more than 2.8 tons of piperonal had been stopped; however, no additional details were provided.

(b) Safrole, safrole-rich oils and isosafrole

Licit trade

96. During the reporting period, eight exporting countries sent via PEN Online to 15 importing countries 37 pre-export notifications for shipments of safrole and safrole-rich oils, with a total volume of 4,000 litres. Though that is about the same trade volume as in the previous three years, it represents a significant decline from the peak reached in 2011. Unlike the situation years earlier, only a small portion of the traded safrole was in the form of safrole-rich oils. During the reporting period, there was no pre-export notification for isosafrole, an intermediate in the synthesis of MDMA from safrole.

Trafficking

97. As in previous years, very few Governments provided on form D for 2014 information about suspicious and stopped shipments of safrole, safrole-rich oils and isosafrole. In 2014, German authorities reported having prevented two shipments totalling 1,050 litres from entering the country; further details were not provided.

98. Reported seizures of safrole, safrole-rich oils and isosafrole have fluctuated significantly over the years. For 2014, only Australia and Namibia reported on form D seizures of safrole and/or isosafrole. Namibia reported the seizure of 2,100 litres of isosafrole, but information about the circumstances and the origin of the substance had not been provided at the time of writing the present report.

99. According to other sources, however, significant seizures of safrole-rich oils were made in Cambodia in August 2014. The seizures, which took place in different locations, resulted in the recovery of a total of nearly 5,000 litres of safrole-rich oils that had been buried in 140 underground tanks. It is believed that the tanks were buried in 2012, when police had intensified their efforts against the production and sale of safrole-rich oils in Pursat Province of Cambodia. Verification of the information is ongoing.

100. Seizures of safrole and safrole-rich oils continued to be communicated through PICS in 2015. In June 2015, a sophisticated industrial-scale laboratory operation for the illicit manufacture of MDMA was discovered in Ontario, Canada. Acting on information about a suspicious transaction, authorities conducted a search of the company's premises that resulted in the seizure of 1,500 litres of safrole-rich oils; 1,000 kg of helional, a precursor of 3,4-methylenedioxyamphetamine that is not under international control, were also seized. Investigations are under way. These incidents show that closely monitoring legitimate trade transactions at the national and international levels can lead to valuable information indicating illicit activity.

101. In July 2015, 5 tons of unspecified precursors of amphetamine-type stimulants were seized in a warehouse in Bolikhamxay Province of the Lao People's Democratic Republic, near that country's border with Viet Nam.

3. Use of non-scheduled substances and other trends in the illicit manufacture of amphetamine-type stimulants

102. Illicit manufacture of amphetamine-type stimulants has diversified significantly in recent years. The precursors of amphetamine-type stimulants now include chemicals available off the shelf (such as benzaldehyde, nitroethane, methylamine and a range of reagents), as well as a number of unusual chemicals that may be made on demand with a view to circumventing existing controls ("designer" precursors). In the light of the constantly and rapidly changing array of chemicals being used in illicit drug manufacture, **INCB wishes to remind Governments of the importance of sharing information about non-scheduled chemicals, their sources, the modi operandi** of traffickers and the actual or suspected use of non-scheduled chemicals in illicit drug manufacture. Such information-sharing should start at the national level, when a company receives a suspicious order and reports it to the competent national authorities; and such information should also be shared at the international level, to prevent traffickers from exploiting weak links elsewhere. PICS provides an opportunity for the early sharing of such information worldwide.

(a) Pre-precursors of amphetamine and methamphetamine

103. The countries that reported on form D for 2014 substances not included in Table I or II of the 1988 Convention but identified as having been used in the illicit manufacture of amphetamine or methamphetamine included Mexico and several European countries (Czech Republic, Denmark, Estonia, Germany, Hungary and Russian Federation).

104. Of those substances, the one most frequently reported in 2014 was benzaldehyde, a pre-precursor of amphetamine and methamphetamine, although the amounts remained small, totalling just 12 kg, in Denmark, Germany, Hungary and the Russian Federation. Benzaldehyde was typically seized together with nitroethane in clandestine amphetamine laboratories. Estonia reported a single seizure of nearly 16 kg of 1-phenyl-2-nitropropene, the reaction product of benzaldehyde and nitroethane, in an illicit amphetamine laboratory. A record single seizure of 10 tons of benzaldehyde was made in Australia in the financial year 2013/14;[26, 27] however, no further details have been made available. In 2015, Austria reported through PICS the seizure of 270 litres of benzaldehyde and 250 litres of nitroethane in a clandestine laboratory. **INCB commends those Governments that provided details of seizures of non-scheduled substances on form D, and it wishes to remind all other Governments that the provision of such information is an obligation under article 12, paragraph 12 (b), of the 1988 Convention and critical to establishing new trends.**

105. Mexico reported seizures amounting to nearly 63 tons of ethyl phenylacetate, an ester of phenylacetic acid: 58.5 tons of the substance were found on a truck and about 4 tons were found abandoned on a beach. In continuation of a trend observed during the previous year, none of the seizures were made at international borders, suggesting

---

[26] In Australia, the financial year begins on 1 July and ends the following year on 30 June.

[27] Australian Crime Commission, *Illicit Drug Data Report 2013-14.*

that the control measures introduced in Mexico and in the countries in which, in the past, consignments of that substance had originated, are having the desired effect. In addition, Mexican authorities reported having seized in clandestine laboratories varying amounts of other pre-precursors of P-2-P, including benzyl cyanide, 2-phenylacetamide and phenylethyl alcohol. Most of those chemicals, namely the derivatives of phenylacetic acid, have been under national control in Mexico since November 2009.

106. As in the previous five years, Mexico also reported seizures of tartaric acid. In 2014, more than 2.8 tons of the substance were seized in clandestine methamphetamine laboratories in Mexico, which represents a continuation of the decline from the peak level of 2011. Tartaric acid is used to enrich the more potent form of methamphetamine manufactured using P-2-P-based methods, thus achieving potency levels comparable to or higher than the potency levels of methamphetamine manufactured from ephedrine or pseudoephedrine, depending on the level of sophistication of the laboratory.

107. In response to the tightening of controls on precursors, including controls on pharmaceutical preparations containing ephedrine and pseudoephedrine (in 2012) and on *Ephedra* plant material (in 2013), China has continued to identify the use of non-scheduled chemicals in illicit drug manufacture.[28] In particular, it is now evident that 2-bromopropiophenone is used to illicitly synthesize ephedrine, as it has been found that more than 50 per cent of the crystalline methamphetamine on illicit markets in that country have been synthesized from that substance. After 2-bromopropiophenone came under national control in May 2014, a number of manufacturers and operators in China were closed down and more than 20 tons of the substance was seized. In 2014, for the first time, a person was arrested in China for illicitly manufacturing synthetic ephedrine.

108. A record seizure of a non-scheduled "designer" precursor of methamphetamine was reported by German authorities: 2.9 tons of "chloro(pseudo)ephedrine"[14] hydrochloride, seized in a warehouse in Leipzig, Germany, in November 2014. Investigations are still ongoing but it has been confirmed that the seized substance was produced specifically at the request of the main suspect in Switzerland and delivered to Germany. A total of 600 grams of the substance, originating in Germany, was reported seized in the Czech Republic, and nearly 400 grams of the substance was reported through PICS in New Zealand. **INCB wishes to remind Governments of**

the possibility of traffickers approaching legitimate industry for customized synthesis of non-scheduled intermediates and the need to alert industry to that possibility. A list of key substitute chemicals, including the relevant extended definitions covering a range of derivatives and chemically related substances, is available to competent national authorities in the limited international special surveillance list of non-scheduled substances, as part of the information package on the control of precursors, on the secure website of INCB.

109. Methylamine (monomethylamine) is a chemical required for the illicit manufacture of not only methamphetamine but also MDMA and several new psychoactive substances. Incidents involving methylamine were reported on form D for 2014 by the authorities of five countries (Germany, Malaysia, Mexico, Netherlands and United States). Seizures of the substance in Malaysia (22.5 litres) and Mexico (more than 3,700 litres) were made in clandestine methamphetamine laboratories; the seizure location in the United States was not provided. Seizures of the substance in the Netherlands amounted to more than 9,500 litres and were made in three unspecified clandestine laboratories; the seizures reported on form D were largely a confirmation of information communicated in real time through PICS in 2014.

110. Germany reported three attempts by traffickers to obtain a total of 32.1 tons of methylamine. In two instances, companies in Belgium and the Netherlands tried to obtain methylamine in Germany; as the end use was either suspicious or not provided, both shipments were denied and the authorities of the countries of destination were informed. The third incident involved an attempted theft of the substance.

111. Seizures of methylamine also continued in 2015, with 10 incidents in which more than 6,500 litres of the substance was seized, communicated through PICS by the Netherlands alone. In one of the laboratories, more than 60 tons of chemicals were seized. Methylamine was the subject of Operation MMA (see para. 38 above).

112. A number of countries reported on form D for 2014 seizures of other non-scheduled chemicals essential to the illicit manufacture of amphetamine and methamphetamine. Chinese authorities reported seizures of thionyl chloride, a chemical required for manufacturing methamphetamine from ephedrine and pseudoephedrine using a method common in South-East Asia; seizures of thionyl chloride in China amounted to nearly 18.5 tons in 2014, compared with 14 tons in 2013. Thailand reported seizures of sodium cyanide amounting to 5.5 tons at its border with Myanmar, and it is assumed that the substance

---

[28] National Narcotics Control Commission of China, *Annual Report on Drug Control in China 2015* (Beijing, 2015).

had been intended for use in illicit methamphetamine manufacture; further details, including information on the origin of the seized sodium cyanide, were not provided.

113. Significant seizures of non-scheduled chemicals associated with a P-2-P-based method for manufacturing amphetamine and methamphetamine known as the Leuckart method were reported by the Netherlands (17.7 tons of formamide and 4,000 litres of formic acid), Peru (nearly 48 tons of formic acid) and Poland (13 kg of formamide, 60 kg of formic acid and 1 kg of ammonium formate). Seizures of non-scheduled chemicals used in modifications of methamphetamine manufacturing methods based on the use of ephedrines were reported by several countries, the largest amounts being reported by the Czech Republic (4.1 tons of iodine and 740 kg of red phosphorus), followed by the Philippines (200 kg of iodine and nearly 400 kg of red phosphorus); in all the other reporting countries combined, seizures of iodine, as well as red phosphorus, amounted to less than 20 kg.

114. Authorities in New Zealand reviewed the modi operandi of those engaged in illicit methamphetamine manufacture and concluded that they obtained other non-scheduled yet essential precursors, including hypophosphorous acid, iodine, potassium iodide and potassium iodate, through a range of methods such as purchasing from legitimate suppliers within the country, stealing from suppliers' premises or from trucks in transit, and direct (often online) purchasing from international vendors.

115. Seizures of a variety of non-scheduled pre-precursors of amphetamine and methamphetamine continued to be communicated through PICS in 2015. They were typically found in illicit laboratories, often in the Netherlands. One seizure in the Netherlands involved 95 kg of the sodium salt of P-2-P glycidic acid, a pre-precursor first identified in the United Kingdom in 2012 that can be converted into P-2-P at a practical ratio of about 2 to 1.

(b) Pre-precursors of 3,4-methylenedioxymethamphetamine (MDMA) and related "ecstasy"-type drugs

116. The methyl ester and sodium salt of 3,4-MDP-2-P methyl glycidate were seized in Europe in 2014, continuing a trend that started in 2010. Seizures of the sodium salt were reported by Belgium (1.74 tons), the Netherlands (2.8 tons) and Spain (1 ton); the type of derivative was not specified in the seizures in Germany (1.25 tons) and Romania (less than 1 kg). In cases where information was provided about the origin or the intended destination of the seized non-scheduled substance, China was cited as the country of origin and the Netherlands was cited as the intended country of destination.

117. Germany also reported a seizure of a small amount of 3,4-(methylenedioxy)phenylacetonitrile, which can be used to synthesize 3,4-MDP-2-P, a substance used to manufacture MDMA (commonly known as "ecstasy"), just as benzyl cyanide can be used to synthesize P-2-P, a substance used to manufacture amphetamine or methamphetamine. Thus, 3,4-(methylenedioxy)phenylacetonitrile is the "ecstasy" equivalent of benzyl cyanide.

118. Seizures of 3,4-MDP-2-P glycidic acid derivatives continued in 2015. One seizure at the Romanian seaport of Constanta involved the shipment of 1 ton of the sodium salt of 3,4-MDP-2-P methyl glycidic acid, communicated via PICS. The shipment had originated in China and had been destined for the Netherlands.

119. **In the light of the variety of non-scheduled "designer" precursors that are being encountered by regulatory and law enforcement authorities, INCB wishes once again to draw attention to the challenges that some of the new chemical derivatives may pose to forensic laboratories regarding the identification of such precursors. For example, the inadvertent generation of analytical artefacts during laboratory analysis may suggest the presence of a controlled primary precursor such as P-2-P or 3,4-MDP-2-P when in fact the analysed sample was the sodium salt of the glycidic acid derivative.**

B. Substances used in the illicit manufacture of cocaine

1. Potassium permanganate

120. Potassium permanganate is an oxidizing agent used in the illicit manufacture of cocaine. A minimum of about 145 tons of the substance is required annually for illicit cocaine manufacture in the three coca-producing countries.[29] While those countries account for only a very limited proportion of legitimate international trade in potassium permanganate, a relatively large proportion of global seizures of potassium permanganate continues to be

---

[29] This figure is based on average low-end estimates by UNODC of the potential manufacture of 100 per cent pure cocaine in the period 2010-2013, published in the *World Drug Report 2015* (annex I), and the approximate quantities of potassium permanganate required (see annex IV to the present report). Note that potential cocaine hydrochloride production in Colombia increased by about 52 per cent in 2014 compared with 2013 (UNODC and Government of Colombia, *Colombia: Coca Cultivation Survey 2014* (Bogota, July 2015), p. 11).

reported by them. In the absence of any recent significant diversions of potassium permanganate from legitimate international trade and other indicators suggesting that cocaine continues to be highly oxidized, it appears that the potassium permanganate that is used in illicit cocaine manufacture has been mainly diverted from domestic distribution channels into illicit channels or has been illicitly manufactured.

Licit trade

121. During the reporting period, the authorities of 31 exporting countries notified their counterparts in 125 importing countries of plans to export 1,357 shipments of potassium permanganate totalling more than 25,500 tons; the corresponding figures in previous years were about the same. As in previous years, the three coca-producing countries — Bolivia (Plurinational State of), Colombia and Peru — accounted for less than 1 per cent of all the imports of potassium permanganate for which notifications were sent through the PEN Online system.

122. Spain was the only country reporting on form D stopped shipments of potassium permanganate — a total of 18 shipments of the substance, amounting to about 26 tons, intended for various countries of destination. Many of those shipments appear to have been stopped for administrative reasons.

123. The pronounced effect of chemical control on cocaine availability was recently demonstrated in a study on the impact of federal cocaine chemical regulations on the availability of cocaine in the United States during the period 1989-2006. The findings of the study, which were consistent with the findings of similar research on methamphetamine and heroin, showed precursor control to be the first policy with such a demonstrated breadth of impact across major illicit drugs.[30]

Trafficking

124. In 2014, as in previous years, global seizures of potassium permanganate were dominated by seizures made in Colombia, where more than 166 tons of the substance was seized, the largest amount seized in six years. Eleven other countries reported on form D for 2014 seizures of potassium permanganate totalling 7.5 tons; seizures in excess of 1 ton were reported by Peru (2.7 tons), China (2.1 tons), Bolivia (Plurinational State of) (1.5 tons) and Venezuela (Bolivarian Republic of) (1.12 tons in

two instances involving illicit laboratories). Additional seizures of potassium permanganate were also communicated through PICS in 2015.

125. About 99 per cent of global seizures of potassium permanganate were made in countries in South America, including the three coca-producing countries (Bolivia (Plurinational State of), Colombia and Peru). Seizures reported by Colombia did not include seizures of potassium permanganate in the form of solutions, as the concentrations are usually not known. Authorities of Colombia, Ecuador and Venezuela (Bolivarian Republic of) indicated that the substance had originated in their countries, which represents a continuation of the overall trend of the previous few years whereby potassium permanganate diverted from domestic distribution channels is used to feed illicit cocaine processing in South America. Colombian authorities also continued to dismantle laboratories illicitly manufacturing potassium permanganate from chemicals not under international control (see para. 129 below).

126. There was no information to substantiate a further spread of coca bush cultivation outside the three coca-producing countries, unlike the situation in 2013, when a small illicit coca bush cultivation site was detected in Panama, and in 2014, when illicit coca bush cultivation sites were discovered in Mexico near that country's border with Guatemala. **Nonetheless, INCB wishes to reiterate its warning about the possibility of illicit coca bush cultivation, cocaine manufacture and related precursor trafficking spreading to countries previously not affected by such illicit activity and the need to address such developments collectively at the regional and international levels.**

2. Use of non-scheduled substances and other trends in the illicit manufacture of cocaine

127. Several countries in Latin America and elsewhere reported seizures of a variety of chemicals not under international control but used in the processing, refinement (after trafficking) or adulteration of cocaine. Those chemicals include solvents used for the extraction of cocaine base from coca leaves and for the conversion of cocaine base into cocaine hydrochloride, chemicals used in the illicit manufacture of internationally controlled precursors, and chemicals used for improving the efficiency of cocaine processing by reducing the volume of chemicals needed and/or the processing time. Several of these alternative chemicals that are not under international control (but are often under national control in the countries concerned) are known to have been used in illicit drug manufacture for many years and have partly replaced some chemicals under international control, in particular

---

[30] James K. Cunningham, et al., "US federal cocaine essential ('precursor') chemical regulation impacts on US cocaine availability: an intervention time-series analysis with temporal replication", *Addiction*, vol. 110 (2015), pp. 805-820.

substances in Table II of the 1988 Convention. Furthermore, improved processing techniques, especially related to illicit cocaine manufacture, and recycling and reuse have resulted in reduced requirements for acids and solvents in Table II. **To improve knowledge of the chemicals actually being used and their sources, INCB encourages Governments to use form D to report details of seizures of, and describe links between, the various alternative (scheduled and non-scheduled) substances.**

128. Significant amounts of such chemicals were reported on form D for 2014 by the authorities of the three coca-producing countries and other countries in South America, as well as the authorities of Spain. In the majority of cases, those chemicals were reported to have been obtained from domestic sources. For example, Colombia seized in almost 700 incidents more than 3,000 tons of urea, a substance used in the illicit manufacture of ammonia and/or used as fertilizer in coca bush cultivation.[31] The seizure of more than one ton of urea was also reported in 2014 by the authorities of the Bolivia (Plurinational State of) Bolivia (3.2 tons), Peru (12 tons) and Venezuela (Bolivarian Republic of) (30 tons).

129. In 2014, Colombia also reported having seized a total of 123 tons of manganese dioxide at 10 illicit potassium permanganate manufacturing sites and about 4.5 tons of potassium manganate at 13 illicit potassium permanganate manufacturing sites. In all cases, the seized substances were reported to have originated in Colombia. Neither manganese dioxide or potassium manganate is in Table I or II of the 1988 Convention, but both are in the INCB limited international special surveillance list of non-scheduled substances and are under national control in Colombia. Seizures of precursors of potassium permanganate in Colombia continued in 2015: in July, a seizure of 3 tons of potassium manganate was made in a single illicit laboratory; in the same laboratory, almost 3.5 tons of potassium permanganate was also seized.

130. Seizures of sodium metabisulphite, a reducing agent used to standardize the oxidation level of cocaine base from different sources prior to further processing, were reported in 2014 by the authorities of Colombia (54 tons), Bolivia (Plurinational State of) (16.2 tons) and Venezuela (Bolivarian Republic of) (1,860 kg). Seizures of this substance by Bolivian and Colombian authorities increased steadily during the past few years. Seizures of small amounts of the substance were also reported in Ecuador (20.8 kg) and Spain (4 kg). The seizures typically occurred in illicit laboratories. Incidents involving sodium metabisulphite continued in 2015, with three incidents in Colombia, totalling 1,465 kg, communicated via PICS.

---

[31] Urea can also be used to produce explosives.

131. Another chemical used to increase the efficiency of cocaine processing is calcium chloride, a drying agent for solvents, used in the conversion of cocaine into cocaine hydrochloride; it is also used in the recycling and reusing of solvents. Varying amounts of calcium chloride have been reported on form D by a number of countries over the years. In 2014, seizures involving several tons of calcium chloride were reported on form D by Bolivian authorities (13 tons) and Colombian authorities (28 tons); and Ecuadorian and Venezuelan authorities reported having seized small amounts. The extent of solvent recycling is evident from data from the Plurinational State of Bolivia (see figure III).

Figure III.   Number of illicit laboratories dismantled in the Plurinational State of Bolivia, by type of laboratory, 2004-2014

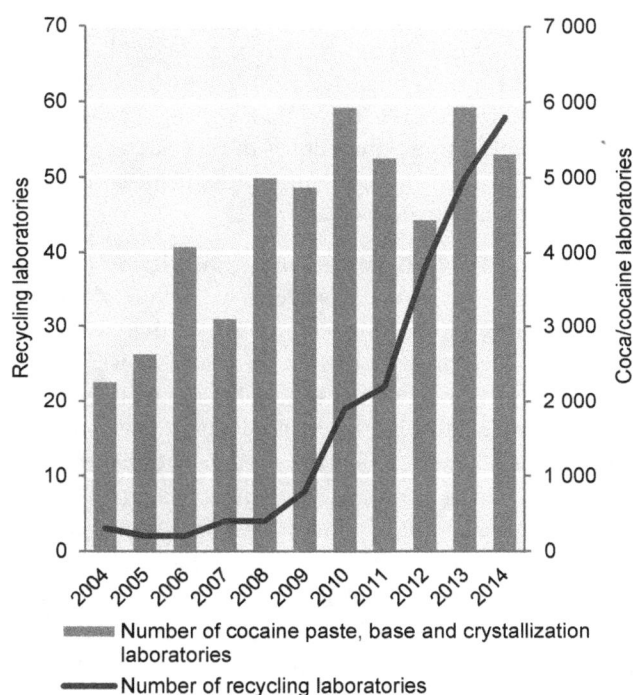

Number of cocaine paste, base and crystallization laboratories

Number of recycling laboratories

Source: United Nations Office on Drugs and Crime and Plurinational State of Bolivia, *Estado Plurinacional de Bolivia: Monitoreo de Cultivos de Coca 2014* (2015)

132. Latin American countries also continued to report significant amounts of various acetate solvents, such as ethyl acetate, butyl acetate, isopropyl and *n*-propyl acetate, isopropyl alcohol and methyl isobutyl ketone, all of which are known to have been used for many years in illicit cocaine processing as substitutes for solvents in Table II of the 1988 Convention. The particular solvents and the amounts reported on form D reflect cocaine manufacturing preferences that are often associated with different groups of illegal operators. Forensic analysis can be used to

determine the differences in the solvents used in the final crystallization, which helps to identify links between samples of seized cocaine hydrochloride and to establish processing trends, and can thus provide valuable information for regulatory authorities.

133. Incidents involving non-scheduled chemicals used for illicit cocaine processing continued to be communicated through PICS in 2015.

C. Acids and solvents in Table II of the 1988 Convention that are used in the illicit manufacture of narcotic drugs and psychotropic substances

134. Acids and solvents in Table II of the 1988 Convention are required throughout various stages of nearly all illicit drug manufacture. Given the average scale of illicit heroin and cocaine processing operations compared with the average scale of illicit synthetic drug manufacture operations, the largest amounts of those acids and solvents were seized in countries in which plant-based drug manufacture is known to occur.

135. A total of 27 countries and territories reported on form D for 2014 seizures of solvents in Table II of the 1988 Convention (acetone, ethyl ether, methyl ethyl ketone and toluene). The largest seizures of those solvents were reported by Myanmar (almost 2.5 million litres of toluene) and Colombia (460,000 litres of acetone). Myanmar also reported having seized the largest amount of hydrochloric acid (1.6 million litres) and sulphuric acid (6.7 million litres), followed by the amounts of seizures of those two acids in China and in coca-producing countries. Acids in Table II were reported to have been seized in 31 countries and territories in 2014. **INCB commends Governments for having provided detailed data on seizures of substances in Table II of the 1988 Convention. The Board notes that in many cases where information about the origin of a seized chemical was provided, the chemical had been obtained from a domestic source; Governments are therefore encouraged to take measures to address the diversion of chemicals from domestic distribution channels.**

136. Information on acids and solvents in Table II of the 1988 Convention also continued to be communicated through PICS. Over the years, the proportion of PICS incidents involving substances in Table II has increased (see figure IV); it is likely that that development is linked to the increase in the number of illicit laboratories on which information is communicated through PICS.

Figure IV. Proportion of incidents communicated via the Precursors Incident Communication System and involving substances in Table II of the 1988 Convention, by quarter, 2012-2015

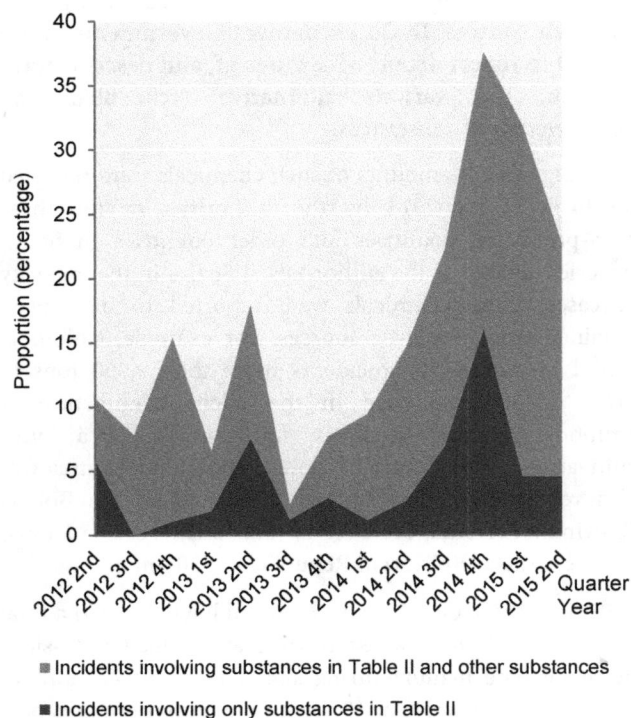

■ Incidents involving substances in Table II and other substances

■ Incidents involving only substances in Table II

D. Substances used in the illicit manufacture of heroin

1. Acetic anhydride

137. Acetic anhydride is the key substance used in the illicit manufacture of heroin. It is also required in the illicit manufacture of methamphetamine or amphetamine in instances where the immediate precursor P-2-P is illicitly derived from phenylacetic acid or phenylacetic acid derivatives (see annex IV). While seizures of acetic anhydride in Afghanistan and neighbouring countries are typically associated with illicit heroin manufacturing attempts, seizures of the substance in Mexico and neighbouring countries used to be largely related to the use of phenylacetic acid derivatives in the illicit manufacture of methamphetamine. However, they may also be attributed to illicit heroin manufacture, as Mexico has continued to be a source of heroin in the Americas and estimates of illicit opium poppy cultivation in Mexico have continued to be high.

138. In spite of the fact that Myanmar is the country with the second largest total area under illicit opium poppy cultivation and the second largest potential opium production, there continues to be a lack of information

reported by that country and other countries in East and South-East Asia on seizures of acetic anhydride and other chemicals required to process opium into morphine and, subsequently, heroin.

Licit trade

139. Acetic anhydride continued to be one of the most frequently traded substances in Table I of the 1988 Convention. During the reporting period, authorities of 25 exporting countries and territories used the PEN Online system to provide over 1,493 pre-export notifications for international trade in acetic anhydride.[32] The shipments of acetic anhydride were destined for 86 importing countries and territories and involved a total of 352 million litres of the substance.

140. The situation with regard to the diversion of acetic anhydride is similar to the situation with regard to the diversion of potassium permanganate: there have not been any known diversions of acetic anhydride from international trade in recent years. However, Operation Eagle Eye, which was conducted by the INCB Precursor Task Force from July 2013 to May 2014, confirmed that the control measures applied to domestic trade in and distribution and end use of acetic anhydride lagged behind those applied in international trade.

141. Attempts to divert acetic anhydride from international trade continued during the reporting period, though there were relatively few attempts. There were two unsuccessful attempts by a company located in the Kurdistan region of Iraq to obtain acetic anhydride through intermediaries in Spain. The competent national authorities of Iraq informed the Spanish authorities that the company in question was not authorized to import the substance, and subsequently the Spanish authorities stopped the shipments. In December 2014, authorities in Pakistan objected through PEN Online to a shipment of 3,700 litres of acetic anhydride from China. Investigations revealed that the company did not reside at the address provided; investigations are ongoing.

142. INCB has previously expressed concern over the insufficiency and inconsistency of information about the magnitude and patterns of licit manufacture of and trade in acetic anhydride, and it continues to believe that domestic transactions involving the substance are not sufficiently monitored in many countries. **INCB therefore encourages Governments to consider the registration of all companies that are in any way involved in acetic anhydride manufacture, trade, distribution or end use.**

INCB wishes once more to encourage Governments of countries in which acetic anhydride and other scheduled substances are manufactured to report accurate, complete and up-to-date details of such manufacture in accordance with Economic and Social Council resolution 1995/20.

Trafficking

143. Of the 13 countries and territories that reported seizures of acetic anhydride on form D for 2014, only Afghanistan, China and Mexico reported the seizure of more than 1,000 litres of the substance.

144. The total volume of acetic anhydride seized in Afghanistan in 2014, about 7,750 litres, was just about half the amount reported in 2013, thus continuing a declining trend, at a year-on-year rate of 50 per cent, that had started in 2011, when the total amount seized was about 68,000 litres (see figure V). The reporting of seizures of acetic anhydride in countries neighbouring Afghanistan has been traditionally low, with few exceptions. Tajikistan, Turkmenistan and Uzbekistan have not reported on form D any seizures of acetic anhydride since 2000, while cooperation between the Governments of China and Iran (Islamic Republic of) has resulted in significant amounts of the substance being seized in 2013 by the Chinese authorities (95,000 litres) and the Iranian authorities (16,500 litres).

Figure V. Seizures of acetic anhydride reported on form D by Afghanistan and other countries in West Asia, 2006-2014

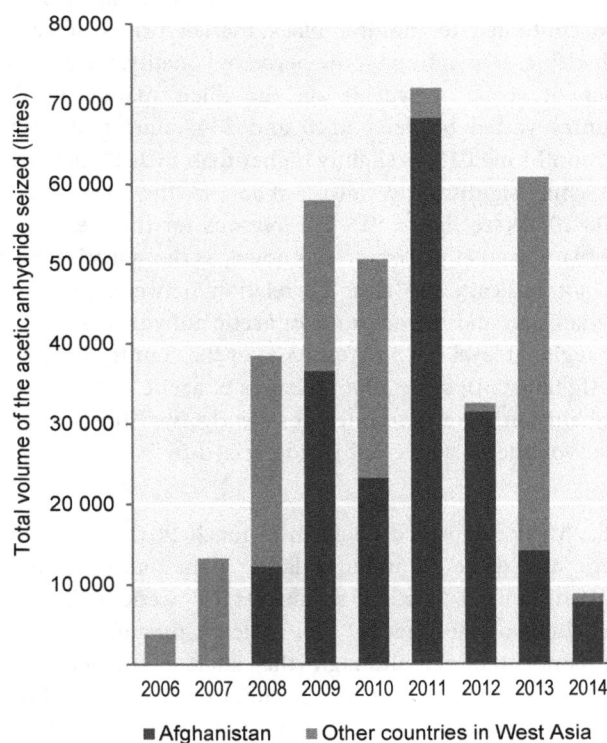

_____

[32] Not including trade between States members of the European Union.

145. According to data provided by Afghanistan on form D for the years 2011-2014, acetic anhydride was smuggled into that country through the Islamic Republic of Iran in over 85 per cent of the cross-border trafficking cases involving the substance and through Pakistan in the remaining 15 per cent of such cases. However, the detection rate of acetic anhydride trafficking across the Afghan border is low. Afghan authorities estimate that less than half of all seizures of acetic anhydride in Afghanistan occur at the border, whereas most of the seizures are made inland, while the substance is being transported from temporary warehouses to illicit heroin manufacturing sites. Intelligence suggests that such temporary warehousing of acetic anhydride is used by traffickers to circumvent any surveillance operations by national law enforcement authorities.

146. To address the problem of decreasing rates for intercepting trafficked precursors, Afghan law enforcement authorities launched two special operations in 2015, focusing on the identification and disruption of domestic transportation of smuggled precursors and on the analysis of data on licit trade from countries identified in the past as being sources of diverted acetic anhydride. Furthermore, in line with the recommendations of Operation Eagle Eye, the Afghan law enforcement authorities reviewed risk indicators used by customs authorities to identify cases of trafficking in acetic anhydride.

147. In 2015, authorities in Afghanistan continued to communicate through PICS seizures of acetic anhydride (total amount seized: over 1,500 litres). The Government also continued to monitor black market prices of acetic anhydride. Depending on the perceived quality, the average price of acetic anhydride on the illicit market in the country varied between $140 and $347 during the first 10 months of 2015 — slightly higher than in 2013 and 2014 but still significantly lower than in the peak years 2008-2010 (see figure VI). The reasons for this decline in the black market price are not known, as the statistical data do not indicate any clear correlation between prices in Afghanistan and the amounts of acetic anhydride seized at the regional level (i.e. in West Asia) or the country level (i.e. in Afghanistan); since 2006, seizures of acetic anhydride in Afghanistan have accounted for nearly two thirds of the total volume of acetic anhydride seized in West Asia (see figure V).

148. Mexico reported on form D for 2014 the seizure of acetic anhydride in amounts larger than those seized in Afghanistan; in Mexico, shipments of acetic anhydride are known to feed the illicit manufacture of methamphetamine, although the illicit manufacture of heroin is also on the rise. The seizure of nearly 13,500 litres of acetic anhydride was reported by Mexico in 2014, twice the amount seized in 2013 but still only about 20 per cent of what was seized in 2011, when seizures of the substance peaked. Seizures of acetic anhydride in China amounted to more than 22,600 litres; the context of those seizures was not provided.

Figure VI. Price of acetic anhydride on the black market in Afghanistan, 2006-2015

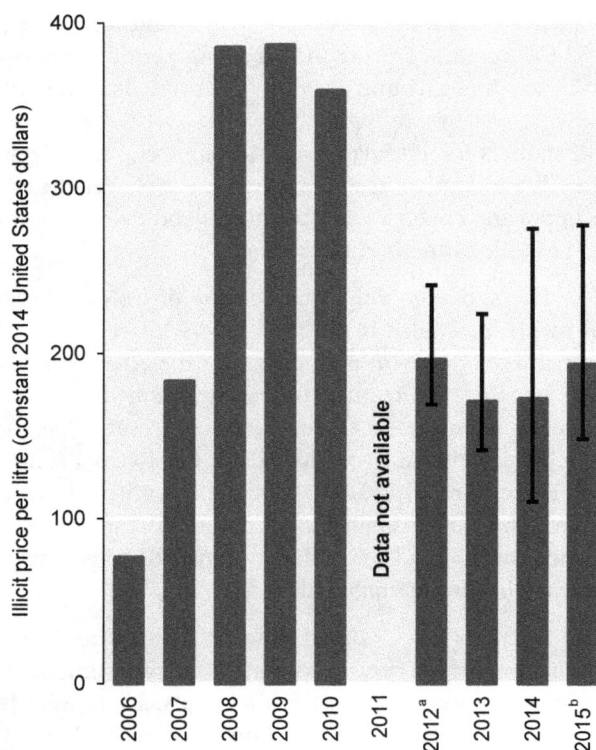

Note: Values represent unweighted average of all samples. Error bars represent the average illicit price range based on the perceived quality of the acetic anhydride in the samples, which were collected and reported beginning in March 2012.

[a] Data for 2012 are for the period from March to December.

[b] Data for 2015 are for the period from January to October.

149. Seizures of acetic anhydride in amounts totalling more than 100 litres were reported on form D for 2014 by Turkey (850 litres), Pakistan (185 litres) and Spain (110 litres). During the reporting period, 12 incidents involving acetic anhydride were communicated via PICS (though some of those incidents related to seizures of the substance that may already have been included in the aggregate totals reported on form D).

150. Seizures of acetic anhydride continued in 2015. The authorities of the Netherlands informed INCB about the theft of a truck transporting 18,000 litres of acetic anhydride to a company based in that country; although the investigation into the theft resulted in the stolen truck being found, the acetic anhydride has not been recovered. In April 2015, Austrian authorities seized 2.2 tons of acetic anhydride;

the circumstances of the seizure, including the modus operandi and the countries involved, were similar to those of other diversion cases investigated in the European Union several years ago. According to information provided by the authorities of the countries involved, the origin of the seized substance was a legitimate company in the Czech Republic and the shipment was destined for a consignee in Slovenia; investigations are ongoing. In the second half of 2015, Iranian customs made two seizures of acetic anhydride totalling more than 28 tons, concealed in transit containers, according to the Iranian Customs Administration. Through PICS, Pakistan communicated four seizures of acetic anhydride in 2015, amounting to over 5,000 litres.

151. INCB has previously noted a lack of information about the sources of chemicals feeding illicit heroin manufacture in Afghanistan. The same is true for other regions affected by illicit opium poppy cultivation and illicit heroin manufacture. In general, there is little or no information about incidents (seizures, diversions, attempted diversions and stopped shipments) and trafficking trends involving acetic anhydride not only in Afghanistan but also in neighbouring countries and worldwide; in cases in which such information is available, it is often very limited, lacking any details on which action can be taken. **INCB therefore encourages all Governments to make every effort to identify the modi operandi of those involved in trafficking in acetic anhydride and to communicate through established channels any relevant details (including information about the sources of that substance). In doing so, Governments should consider communicating possible changes in trafficking routes, concealment methods, modi operandi and trafficking trends, as well as the possible shifting of illicit heroin laboratories to previously unsuspected locations (such laboratories were identified, for example, in Spain in 2013 and 2014).**

2. Use of non-scheduled substances and other trends in the illicit manufacture of heroin

152. The non-scheduled chemicals most frequently associated with illicit heroin processing are ammonium chloride, commonly used in the extraction of morphine from opium, and glacial acetic acid, which has long been suspected of being used: (a) as a cover load, to conceal acetic anhydride contraband; and (b) in the acetylation of morphine to heroin, probably mixed with acetic anhydride. Neither chemical is under international control but both are in the limited international special surveillance list of non-scheduled substances and, according to information available to INCB, are under national control in a number of countries and territories (21 in the case of glacial acetic acid and 8 in the case of ammonium chloride).

153. Four countries reported seizures of ammonium chloride on form D for 2014. The largest seizures were reported by Afghanistan (19.3 tons), followed by Thailand (600 kg) and Mexico and Peru (less than 100 kg each). Seizures of acetic acid were reported by (in descending order of amount seized) Brazil, Mexico, Peru and Argentina; however, no specific reference to illicit heroin manufacture was made in connection with any of the reported seizures of acetic acid. **INCB wishes to acknowledge the provision of information about substances not in Table I or II of the 1988 Convention and encourages all Governments to provide on form D complete and comprehensive information about such substances (in particular, the intended or suspected use of such substances and their sources), with a view to establishing trends and preventing the diversion of those substances worldwide.**

E. Substances used in the illicit manufacture of other narcotic drugs and psychotropic substances

1. Ergot alkaloids and lysergic acid

Licit trade

154. Ergot alkaloids (ergometrine and ergotamine and their salts) are used in the treatment of migraines and as an oxytocic in obstetrics, but there is comparatively limited international trade in those substances. During the reporting period, 17 countries sent pre-export notifications to 48 importing countries for 335 exports of ergot alkaloids totalling nearly 1,340 kg; there was one shipment of lysergic acid.

155. Authorities in the Netherlands informed INCB of significant amounts of ergot alkaloids being delivered from the Czech Republic to an operator in the Netherlands between December 2013 and August 2014 without the required license. Investigations are ongoing. Since December 2014, authorities in the Netherlands, Suriname and Switzerland have cooperated with each other and the Board, to prevent traffickers from misusing a company in Suriname for the diversion of ergot alkaloids. While it appears that two shipments of 1 kg each might have been delivered, further known orders amounting to more than 8 kg over a two-year period will not be delivered, as a result of the cooperation of the authorities concerned. **INCB is aware that there have also been attempts to obtain the chemicals from other exporting countries and therefore invites all Governments to exercise vigilance with regard to orders and shipments of ergot alkaloids.**

Trafficking

156. Available information suggests that lysergic acid diethylamide (LSD) may be making a return, connected with the increasing role of the Internet in supplying drugs, and increasing amounts of LSD being seized in several regions. However, there is limited information about the precursors and methods actually being used for the manufacture of LSD. Also, given the potency of LSD, for which dosages are measured in millionths of a gram, only very small quantities of precursor chemicals are needed to manufacture a significant amount of the drug. Not surprisingly, aggregated annual seizures of the precursor chemicals of LSD reported on form D very rarely exceed a couple of hundred grams. Only three countries reported on form D for 2014 seizures of ergotamine, ergometrine or lysergic acid; the reported total amount seized was less than 60 grams.

2. N-Acetylanthranilic acid and anthranilic acid

Licit trade

157. N-Acetylanthranilic acid and anthranilic acid are precursors used for the illicit manufacture of methaqualone, a sedative-hypnotic that is commonly known as "quaalude" or "mandrax" (former brand names of pharmaceutical products that are no longer licitly manufactured). During the reporting period, there were eight pre-export notifications for amounts totalling 280 grams of N-acetylanthranilic acid. In addition, 42 importing countries were sent pre-export notifications by 11 exporting countries for 312 shipments of anthranilic acid totalling nearly 1,122 tons.

Trafficking

158. Reports of seizures of precursors of methaqualone have always been sporadic. In 2014, China was the only country to report seizures of anthranilic acid; those seizures totalled over 800 kg, which is less than the total amount seized in 2013. There were no seizures of N-acetylanthranilic acid in 2014.

159. INCB has as yet been unable to confirm details regarding an alleged large-scale methaqualone laboratory site in the greater Durban area in South Africa, dismantled in June 2014, including details about the chemicals found at the site and their sources. In the meantime, seizures of "mandrax" tablets, continued to be reported regularly on the official website of the South African Police Service. Likewise the dismantling of "mandrax" laboratories has occasionally been reported on the official police website; however, it appears that those laboratories were processing

"mandrax" powder into tablets and not synthesizing methaqualone from chemical starting materials.

F. Substances not in Table I or II of the 1988 Convention that are used in the illicit manufacture of other narcotic drugs and psychotropic substances, precursors under international control or substances of abuse not under international control

160. In 2014, Governments continued to use form D also to report seizures of a variety of substances not in Table I or II of the 1988 Convention that can be used in the illicit manufacture of other narcotic drugs or psychotropic substances, precursors under international control or substances of abuse not under international control, including new psychoactive substances. Seizures reported in 2014 mostly concerned *gamma*-butyrolactone (GBL) and precursors of ketamine.

1. Precursors of gamma-hydroxybutyric acid

161. GBL is a precursor used in the illicit manufacture of gamma-hydroxybutyric acid (GHB), and it is also ingested and metabolized in the body into GHB; 1,4-butanediol is a pre-precursor of GHB and a precursor of GBL. In 2014, GBL seizures were reported by nine countries, mostly in Europe. Each of those countries reported multiple seizures of GBL totalling less than 50 litres (i.e. the individual seizures were usually small), the exception being the Netherlands, which reported having seized a total of nearly 1,100 litres of the substance, including 1,000 litres in a single seizure at a warehouse. In addition to the GBL seizures made in countries in Europe, such seizures were also made in Australia (370 kg) and the United States (49 kg). Information about the origin of the seized substance and the shipping mode was usually not provided; one country mentioned the use of international courier services.

162. GBL seizures continued to be communicated via PICS in 2015; however, the amounts were usually small. Authorities in Australia and the Netherlands communicated incidents involving GBL seizures in warehouses and illicit laboratories.

2. Precursors of ketamine

163. China is the only country that has regularly reported seizures of ketamine precursors. In 2014, China reported

record seizures of illicitly manufactured precursors of ketamine, including nearly 40 tons of an immediate precursor commonly known as "hydroxylimine" (seizures of which had averaged 8 tons a year since 2010) and more than 70 tons of o-chlorophenyl cyclopentyl ketone, another intermediate in the synthesis of ketamine (seizures of which had not been reported before). "Hydroxylimine" has been under national control in China since mid-2008; o-chlorophenyl cyclopentyl ketone since September 2012.

3. Precursors of other drugs

164. A small amount of 4-methoxy-P-2-P, the non-scheduled equivalent of P-2-P used in the illicit manufacture of para-methoxy-alpha-methylphenethylamine (PMA) and para-methoxymethamphetamine (PMMA), was reported to have been seized in the Netherlands in 2014. The substance was seized in a warehouse, together with other precursors and chemicals, which suggests that a multiple-substance approach was being used.

165. The United States reported on form D for 2014 two incidents involving a total of 20 litres of cyclohexanone, a substance that can be used in the illicit manufacture of phencyclidine and several of its analogues; in the United States, there have occasionally been reports of the dismantling of laboratories used for the illicit manufacture of phencyclidine.

IV. Public-private partnerships: their merits and potential in preventing the diversion of chemicals

166. In its 2014 report on precursors,[33] INCB noted the central role of public-private partnerships and voluntary cooperation with industry in an effective strategy to address chemical diversion and pointed out that those areas needed to receive much greater, systematic attention.

167. Over the past three decades, Governments have adopted and implemented a number of measures in accordance with the 1988 Convention. Those measures have principally focused on preventing substances in Tables I and II of the Convention from being diverted into illicit channels by monitoring their movements in international trade. This has led drug traffickers to change their modi operandi to source the chemicals they need for illicit purposes, in particular for illicit drug manufacture. They are increasingly exploiting vulnerabilities in domestic

trade to obtain substances in Tables I and II or non-scheduled substances that can be easily converted into the required precursors. The rapid pace at which those substances are emerging and the almost infinite number of non-scheduled substances that could potentially be used to replace the traditional precursors are among the challenges that many Governments are facing today. Legislative changes provide long-term solutions; however, their enforcement and administration may often be resource-intensive, and in most cases long periods of time are required for their introduction and thus there are limitations in terms of being able to ensure the timely and adequate prevention of the diversion of precursors.

168. This is where the concept of adopting strategies based on voluntary public-private partnerships that supplement the required controls has an increasingly important role to play. The concept is based on shared goals and responsibility and formalized through agreements such as memorandums of understanding, and such strategies provide a number of tangible benefits to both the public sector and the private sector. However, the success of any voluntary mechanism depends on the mutual goodwill, trust and respect of the parties involved. As most of the commercial transactions involving precursor chemicals are legitimate and conducted by bona fide companies as part of their daily business activity, additional legislative controls could potentially place an unnecessary administrative burden on the public and private sectors. The voluntary public-private partnerships, through their speed of response and flexibility, therefore provide effective solutions to address the misuse of non-scheduled chemicals (including "designer" precursors, precursors used to manufacture new psychoactive substances, and off-the-shelf and custom-made chemicals) and the diversion of, and trafficking in, scheduled chemicals at the domestic level.

169. Considering that diversion can and does happen at all stages of the distribution chain, the extent of participation or involvement of private sector stakeholders should not be limited only to manufacturing countries and the chemical industry. Instead, the involvement of all relevant areas of business should be sought, including but not limited to the manufacturing industry, distributors, traders, shippers and end users. The involvement of all relevant sectors of industry should also be sought, including the fine and speciality chemical industries, the pharmaceutical industry and the flavour, fragrance, cosmetics, and food and beverage industries. Thus, all relevant private stakeholders should be engaged in the voluntary framework at the national level. Chemical industry and other associations should also be involved. This will ensure that domestic control and alert systems are able to do what they were designed to do.

---

[33] E/INCB/2014/4, paras. 21 (a) and 77.

170. Although the concept of cooperation with industry has its roots in article 12, paragraph 9 (a), of the 1988 Convention, which requires parties to establish and maintain a system to monitor international trade in substances in Tables I and II in close cooperation with manufacturers, importers, exporters, wholesalers and retailers, it has not yet been implemented to its full potential. While some Governments have had years of experience and obtained positive results in the form of stopped shipments, others have not yet done so; even in countries with a long history of cooperation with industry, there is room to improve cooperation at lower levels of the distribution chain and in relation to non-scheduled chemicals.

171. Another advantage of public-private partnerships that does not often come to mind is their capacity to manage rogue or intractable players within an industry and address unacceptable activity, i.e. activity not in compliance with the code of practice. In many instances, such an agreed code defining the conditions of manufacture, distribution and use of substances at risk of diversion provides the industry with an effective means of self-regulation.

172. To assist Governments in establishing or improving voluntary cooperative mechanisms with the industries concerned, the Board has made available the following written material, which provides practical guidance and includes the main principles underlying such a concept:[34]

(a) *Guidelines for a Voluntary Code of Practice for the Chemical Industry* (published in 2009);

(b) "Practical notes for implementing the International Narcotics Control Board guidelines for a voluntary code of practice for the chemical industry" (published in 2015);

(c) "Development and implementation of a Voluntary Code of Practice for the chemical industry formalized through a memorandum of understanding between government and the private sector: Quick guide", which summarizes the main steps for developing and implementing public-private partnerships and a voluntary code of practice for the chemical industry; and a model memorandum of understanding intended to serve as a basis on which Governments and the chemical industry can develop or enhance voluntary partnerships;

(d) Limited international special surveillance list of non-scheduled substances (published in 1998 and regularly updated by the Board since then).

173. The Board believes that the limited international special surveillance list and similar voluntary monitoring lists are useful tools for proactively addressing the challenges posed by non-scheduled chemicals and substitute chemicals. This applies especially if those lists are expanded in a generic manner — that is, if they go beyond merely listing individual substances and introduce extended definitions that include chemically related substances that can be converted into one of the scheduled precursors by readily applicable means and thus can be used as substitutes for substances in Tables I and II of the 1988 Convention. The chemical industry is well suited to grasping these technical concepts and acting responsibly, as the first line of defence, when it comes to proactively identifying suspicious orders of scheduled and non-scheduled chemicals, notifying regulatory authorities about those orders and thus preventing diversions.

174. To increase the awareness of the merits of voluntary public-private partnership, since 2013 the Board has organized a number of events during which the concept of cooperation between industry and government was discussed in depth and concrete measures and recommendations were adopted.

175. In December 2013, a conference entitled Precursor Control in Asia: Addressing the Challenges was held in Bangkok. Some 100 government officials and experts participated in the conference, discussing ways to further develop cooperation between industry and government, aimed at preventing the use of precursors and other chemicals in illicit drug manufacture. The participants agreed on, among other things, the need to develop practical measures for implementing the INCB *Guidelines for a Voluntary Code of Practice for the Chemical Industry*, as well as codes of conduct and memorandums of understanding.

176. In April 2014, a workshop entitled "Enhancing chemical industry-government cooperation through partnership" was organized by INCB and hosted by the Ministry of the Interior of Bahrain in Manama. The workshop resulted in the adoption of a model memorandum of understanding that can be adapted to specific country needs. The model memorandum of understanding is another part of the written material made available by the Board to provide practical guidance to Governments (see para. 172 above).

177. In April 2015, at the international conference entitled Precursor Chemicals and New Psychoactive Substances, held in Bangkok, a segment of the conference was dedicated to industry-government cooperation. The participants adopted, as part of the outcome document of the

_____

[34] The INCB secretariat will provide the material to competent national authorities upon request; the material is also available on the secure website of the Board.

conference, a series of recommendations related to industry-government cooperation. Those recommendations included building relationships with industry to develop and establish voluntary partnerships formalized by the signing of memorandums of understanding, as well as enhancing already existing relationships with chemical industry representatives to improve the reporting and investigation of suspicious orders and enquiries.

178. The Board, in line with its mandate, stands ready to continue supporting Governments in their efforts to establish and implement such memorandums of understanding and similar cooperation agreements and, in cooperation with the private sector, to prevent the diversion of precursors.

V. Conclusions

179. The INCB report on precursors is aimed at providing Governments with a comprehensive overview and analysis of the precursor control situation worldwide, in terms of the extent of licit trade in precursors, latest trends in precursor trafficking, substitute chemicals and action taken by Governments and the Board. It also provides the Board's observations and recommendations on preventing the diversion of chemicals by traffickers and addressing the latest challenges.[35]

180. It is generally accepted that successes in international precursor control, especially those achieved through PEN Online, the INCB electronic system of pre-export notification, have resulted in decreases in diversions of substances in Tables I and II of the 1988 Convention from international trade. Diversion from domestic distribution channels is now recognized as an important source of those substances. In addition, a range of non-scheduled alternative and substitute chemicals have been used to fill the resulting shortfall in such controlled substances, and many more have the potential to be used as substitutes for such substances.

181. INCB has identified public-private partnerships as one of the most effective measures to address the diversion of both scheduled and non-scheduled alternative chemicals for use in illicit drug manufacture. In chapter IV of the present report, INCB analyses the merits and potential of cooperation between competent authorities and relevant industrial sectors — of all sizes and at all levels; in addition, it invites national authorities to adopt the concept of industry as a critical partner in chemical diversion prevention and to formalize a commitment to such

partnerships, and it invites industry and industry associations to incorporate the principles of chemical diversion prevention into the concept of corporate industry responsibility.

182. Another pillar of effective precursor control in the twenty-first century continues to be the focus on improving national control systems, closing any gaps in those systems and enabling the systems to do what they were meant to do. Lastly, the Board considers it critical for Governments to provide their law enforcement authorities with the legal framework to take appropriate action, where required.[36] For their part, law enforcement authorities must pay more attention to precursor chemicals and illicit manufacture; they must investigate seizures, stopped shipments and attempted diversions in order to identify the sources of diversion and the criminal organizations behind those activities and to share their findings with relevant authorities throughout the world, thereby preventing future diversions based on similar modi operandi.

183. The present report reconfirms that the extent of information-sharing, especially on alternative and substitute chemicals and the corresponding manufacturing methods, continues to be incomplete or not timely enough. INCB therefore wishes to remind Governments that the sharing of information on any chemical that is suspected of being used or has been used in illicit drug manufacture, or information on attempts to divert a chemical into illicit channels, is critical to understanding — and addressing — new developments in the diversion of precursor chemicals and the use of chemicals in illicit drug manufacture.

184. Pursuant to article 12, paragraph 12, of the 1988 Convention, annual reporting of the following information through form D (part one) is mandatory:

(a) Information on any substances not included in Table I or II that have been identified as having been used or as being intended for use in the illicit manufacture of drugs or precursors;

(b) Methods of diversion and illicit manufacture.

185. To gather the relevant information at the national level and contribute to global efforts to prevent chemicals from reaching clandestine drug manufacturing laboratories, the Board encourages Governments to consider the following action:

(a) Gather in a more systematic manner information on chemicals encountered in dismantled

---

[35] One of the special topics in chapter II of the INCB annual report for 2015 (E/INCB/2015/1) covers new developments and challenges in precursor control and the way forward.

[36] The 1988 Convention provides guidance on developing national legislation to that effect for substances in Tables I and II and, in combination with article 13, for non-scheduled chemicals.

clandestine laboratories, including labels of containers found and any information that might help to establish the source of the chemicals;

(b)   Do advocacy with and encourage private sector partners (i.e. partners in industry) to report to the relevant authorities all suspicious orders of scheduled and non-scheduled chemicals, even in cases where such orders have been denied; and report such orders to INCB, with a view to preventing the diversion of such chemicals elsewhere.

186. The participants in the international conference entitled Precursor Chemicals and New Psychoactive Substances, held in Bangkok in April 2015, adopted an outcome document aimed at taking the above-mentioned considerations to the next level by proposing measures to address the misuse of scheduled and non-scheduled precursors and new psychoactive substances. INCB welcomes the outcome document and encourages all Governments to build on it and use the upcoming session of the Commission on Narcotic Drugs and the special session of the General Assembly on the world drug problem to be held in April 2016 to reconfirm their commitment to the fundamental basis of international precursor control and to the spirit of article 12 of the 1988 Convention: international cooperation to prevent chemicals from being available for use in the illicit manufacture of substances of abuse. INCB stands ready to fully support Governments in their efforts.

Glossary

The following terms and definitions have been used in the present report:

"designer" precursor	A chemical that is not available off-the-shelf and may be made by rogue or unsuspecting members of the industry at the request of traffickers (i.e. on demand) with a view to circumventing existing controls
diversion	Transfer of substances from licit to illicit channels
immediate precursor	Precursor that is generally only one reaction step away from the end product
pharmaceutical preparation	Preparation for therapeutic (human or veterinary) use in its finished dosage form that contains precursors present in such a way that they can be used or recovered by readily applicable means; may be presented in their retail packaging or in bulk
pre-precursor	Chemical that can be used to manufacture another precursor; the term usually refers to a non-scheduled chemical used for the illicit manufacture of a controlled precursor
seizure	Prohibiting the transfer, conversion, disposition or movement of property or assuming custody or control of property on the basis of an order issued by a court or a competent authority; may be temporary or permanent (i.e. confiscation); different national legal systems may use different terms
stopped shipment	Shipment permanently withheld because there are reasonable grounds to believe that it may constitute an attempted diversion, as a result of administrative problems or because of other grounds for concern or suspicion
suspended shipment	Shipment temporarily withheld because of administrative inconsistencies or other grounds for concern or suspicion, for which clarification of the veracity of the order and resolution of technical issues are required before the shipment may be released
suspicious order (or suspicious transaction)	Order (or transaction) of questionable, dishonest or unusual character or condition, regarding which there is reason to believe that a substance in Table I or II of the 1988 Convention that is being imported or exported or is transiting is intended for the illicit manufacture of narcotic drugs, psychotropic substances or substances in Table I or II of the Convention

Annexes*

*The annexes are not included in the printed version of the present report but they are available in the CD-ROM version and in the version on the website of the International Narcotics Control Board (www.incb.org).

Annex I

Parties and non-parties to the 1988 Convention, by region, as at 1 November 2015

Note: The date on which the instrument of ratification or accession was deposited is indicated in parentheses.

Region	Parties to the 1988 Convention		Non-parties to the 1988 Convention
Africa	Algeria (9 May 1995)	Eritrea (30 January 2002)	Equatorial Guinea
	Angola (26 October 2005)	Ethiopia (11 October 1994)	Somalia
	Benin (23 May 1997)	Gabon (10 July 2006)	South Sudan
	Botswana (13 August 1996)	Gambia (23 April 1996)	
	Burkina Faso (2 June 1992)	Ghana (10 April 1990)	
	Burundi (18 February 1993)	Guinea (27 December 1990)	
	Cabo Verde (8 May 1995)	Guinea-Bissau (27 October 1995)	
	Cameroon (28 October 1991)	Kenya (19 October 1992)	
	Central African Republic (15 October 2001)	Lesotho (28 March 1995)	
	Chad (9 June 1995)	Liberia (16 September 2005)	
	Comoros (1 March 2000)	Libya (22 July 1996)	
	Congo (3 March 2004)	Madagascar (12 March 1991)	
	Côte d'Ivoire (25 November 1991)	Malawi (12 October 1995)	
	Democratic Republic of the Congo (28 October 2005)	Mali (31 October 1995)	
	Djibouti (22 February 2001)	Mauritania (1 July 1993)	
	Egypt (15 March 1991)	Mauritius (6 March 2001)	

Region	Parties to the 1988 Convention		Non-parties to the 1988 Convention
	Morocco (28 October 1992)	South Africa (14 December 1998)	
	Mozambique (8 June 1998)	Sudan (19 November 1993)	
	Namibia (6 March 2009)	Swaziland (8 October 1995)	
	Niger (10 November 1992)	Togo (1 August 1990)	
	Nigeria (1 November 1989)	Tunisia (20 September 1990)	
	Rwanda (13 May 2002)	Uganda (20 August 1990)	
	Sao Tome and Principe (20 June 1996)	United Republic of Tanzania (17 April 1996)	
	Senegal (27 November 1989)	Zambia (28 May 1993)	
	Seychelles (27 February 1992)	Zimbabwe (30 July 1993)	
	Sierra Leone (6 June 1994)		

Regional total **54**	**51**	**3**
Americas	Antigua and Barbuda (5 April 1993)	Chile (13 March 1990)
	Argentina (10 June 1993)	Colombia (10 June 1994)
	Bahamas (30 January 1989)	Costa Rica (8 February 1991)
	Barbados (15 October 1992)	Cuba (12 June 1996)
	Belize (24 July 1996)	Dominica (30 June 1993)
	Bolivia (Plurinational State of) (20 August 1990)	Dominican Republic (21 September 1993)
	Brazil (17 July 1991)	Ecuador (23 March 1990)
	Canada (5 July 1990)	El Salvador (21 May 1993)

Region	Parties to the 1988 Convention		Non-parties to the 1988 Convention
	Grenada (10 December 1990)	Peru (16 January 1992)	
	Guatemala (28 February 1991)	Saint Kitts and Nevis (19 April 1995)	
	Guyana (19 March 1993)	Saint Lucia (21 August 1995)	
	Haiti (18 September 1995)	Saint Vincent and the Grenadines (17 May 1994)	
	Honduras (11 December 1991)	Suriname (28 October 1992)	
	Jamaica (29 December 1995)	Trinidad and Tobago (17 February 1995)	
	Mexico (11 April 1990)	United States of America (20 February 1990)	
	Nicaragua (4 May 1990)	Uruguay (10 March 1995)	
	Panama (13 January 1994)	Venezuela (Bolivarian Republic of) (16 July 1991)	
	Paraguay (23 August 1990)		

Regional total			
35	35		0
Asia	Afghanistan (14 February 1992)	China (25 October 1989)	State of Palestine
	Armenia (13 September 1993)	Democratic People's Republic of Korea (19 March 2007)	
	Azerbaijan (22 September 1993)	Georgia (8 January 1998)	
	Bahrain (7 February 1990)	India (27 March 1990)	
	Bangladesh (11 October 1990)	Indonesia (23 February 1999)	
	Bhutan (27 August 1990)	Iran (Islamic Republic of) (7 December 1992)	
	Brunei Darussalam (12 November 1993)	Iraq (22 July 1998)	
	Cambodia (2 April 2005)	Israel (20 March 2002)	

Region	Parties to the 1988 Convention		Non-parties to the 1988 Convention
	Japan (12 June 1992)	Qatar (4 May 1990)	
	Jordan (16 April 1990)	Republic of Korea (28 December 1998)	
	Kazakhstan (29 April 1997)	Saudi Arabia (9 January 1992)	
	Kuwait (3 November 2000)	Singapore (23 October 1997)	
	Kyrgyzstan (7 October 1994)	Sri Lanka (6 June 1991)	
	Lao People's Democratic Republic (1 October 2004)	Syrian Arab Republic (3 September 1991)	
	Lebanon (11 March 1996)	Tajikistan (6 May 1996)	
	Malaysia (11 May 1993)	Thailand (3 May 2002)	
	Maldives (7 September 2000)	Timor-Leste (3 June 2014)	
	Mongolia (25 June 2003)	Turkey (2 April 1996)	
	Myanmar (11 June 1991)	Turkmenistan (21 February 1996)	
	Nepal (24 July 1991)	United Arab Emirates (12 April 1990)	
	Oman (15 March 1991)	Uzbekistan (24 August 1995)	
	Pakistan (25 October 1991)	Viet Nam (4 November 1997)	
	Philippines (7 June 1996)	Yemen (25 March 1996)	

Regional total			
47	**46**		**1**
Europe	Albania (27 July 2001)	Belgium[a] (25 October 1995)	
	Andorra (23 July 1999)	Bosnia and Herzegovina (1 September 1993)	
	Austria[a] (11 July 1997)	Bulgaria[a] (24 September 1992)	
	Belarus (15 October 1990)	Croatia[a] (26 July 1993)	

Region	Parties to the 1988 Convention	Non-parties to the 1988 Convention
	Cyprus[a] (25 May 1990)	Monaco (23 April 1991)	
	Czech Republic[b] (30 December 1993)	Montenegro (3 June 2006)	
	Denmark[a] (19 December 1991)	Netherlands[a] (8 September 1993)	
	Estonia[a] (12 July 2000)	Norway (14 November 1994)	
	Finland[a] (15 February 1994)	Poland[a] (26 May 1994)	
	France[a] (31 December 1990)	Portugal[a] (3 December 1991)	
	Germany[a] (30 November 1993)	Republic of Moldova (15 February 1995)	
	Greece[a] (28 January 1992)	Romania[a] (21 January 1993)	
	Holy See (25 January 2012)	Russian Federation (17 December 1990)	
	Hungary[a] (15 November 1996)	San Marino (10 October 2000)	
	Iceland (2 September 1997)	Serbia (3 January 1991)	
	Ireland[a] (3 September 1996)	Slovakia[a] (28 May 1993)	
	Italy[a] (31 December 1990)	Slovenia[a] (6 July 1992)	
	Latvia[a] (25 February 1994)	Spain[a] (13 August 1990)	
	Liechtenstein (9 March 2007)	Sweden[a] (22 July 1991)	
	Lithuania[a] (8 June 1998)	Switzerland (14 September 2005)	
	Luxembourg[a] (29 April 1992)	The former Yugoslav Republic of Macedonia (13 October 1993)	
	Malta[a] (28 February 1996)	Ukraine (28 August 1991)	

Region	Parties to the 1988 Convention		Non-parties to the 1988 Convention
	United Kingdom of Great Britain and Northern Ireland[a] (28 June 1991)	European Union[b] (31 December 1990)	

Regional total			
46	**46**		**0**

Region	Parties to the 1988 Convention		Non-parties to the 1988 Convention
Oceania	Australia (16 November 1992)	New Zealand (16 December 1998)	Kiribati
			Palau
	Cook Islands (22 February 2005)	Niue (16 July 2012)	Papua New Guinea
	Fiji (25 March 1993)	Samoa (19 August 2005)	Solomon Islands
			Tuvalu
	Marshall Islands (5 November 2010)	Tonga (29 April 1996)	
	Micronesia (Federated States of) (6 July 2004)	Vanuatu (26 January 2006)	
	Nauru (12 July 2012)		

Regional total			
16	**11**		**5**

World total			
198	**189**		**9**

[a] State member of the European Union.

[b] Extent of competence: article 12.

Annex II

Annual legitimate requirements for ephedrine, pseudoephedrine, 3,4-methylenedioxyphenyl-2-propanone and 1-phenyl-2-propanone, substances frequently used in the manufacture of amphetamine-type stimulants

1. In its resolution 49/3, entitled "Strengthening systems for the control of precursor chemicals used in the manufacture of synthetic drugs", the Commission on Narcotic Drugs:

(a) Requested Member States to provide to the International Narcotics Control Board annual estimates of their legitimate requirements for 3,4-methylenedioxyphenyl-2-propanone (3,4-MDP-2-P), pseudoephedrine, ephedrine and 1-phenyl-2-propanone (P-2-P) and, to the extent possible, estimated requirements for imports of preparations containing those substances that could be easily used or recovered by readily applicable means;

(b) Requested the Board to provide those estimates to Member States in such a manner as to ensure that such information was used only for drug control purposes;

(c) Invited Member States to report to the Board on the feasibility and usefulness of preparing, reporting and using estimates of legitimate requirements for the precursor chemicals and preparations referred to above in preventing diversion.

2. Pursuant to that resolution, the Board formally invited Governments to prepare estimates of their legitimate requirements for those substances. Those estimates, as reported by Governments, were published, for the first time, in March 2007.

3. The table below reflects the latest data reported by Governments on those four precursor chemicals (and their preparations, as relevant). It is expected that those data will provide the competent authorities of exporting countries with at least an indication of the legitimate requirements of importing countries, thus preventing diversion attempts. Governments are invited to review their requirements as published, amend them as necessary and inform the Board of any required change. The data are current as at 1 November 2015; for updates, see www.incb.org/incb/en/precursors/alrs.html.

Annual legitimate requirements as reported by Governments for imports of ephedrine, pseudoephedrine, 3,4-methylenedioxyphenyl-2-propanone, 1-phenyl-2-propanone and their preparations, as at 1 November 2015
(Kilograms)

Country or territory	Ephedrine	Ephedrine preparations	Pseudoephedrine	Pseudoephedrine preparations	3,4-MDP-2-P[a]	P-2-P[b]
Afghanistan	0	50	0	3 000	0	0
Albania	6	0	4	0	0	0
Algeria	20		17 000		0	1
Argentina	16	0	12 000	125	0	0
Armenia	0	0	0	0	0	0
Ascension Island	0	0	0	0	0	0
Australia	2	11	5 500	1 650	0	0
Austria	122	200	1	1	0	1
Azerbaijan	20		10		0	0
Bahrain	0	0			0	
Bangladesh	200		49 021		0	0
Barbados	200		200	58	0[c]	
Belarus	0	2	25	20	0	0
Belgium	300	200	9 000	8 000	5	5
Belize			P	P	0[c]	
Benin	2	2	8	35	0[c]	
Bhutan	0	0	0	0	0	0
Bolivia (Plurinational State of)	25	1	702	1 340	0	0
Bosnia and Herzegovina	25	1	1 502	1 225	1	1
Botswana	300				0[c]	
Brazil	900[d]		22 000[d]		0	0
Brunei Darussalam	0	5	0	320	0	0
Bulgaria	200	296	25	0	0	0
Cambodia	200	50	300	900	0[c]	
Cameroon	25				0[c]	
Canada	1 330	5	27 900		0	1
Chile	90	0	8 364	82	0	0
China	60 000		200 000		0[c]	
China, Hong Kong SAR	3 050	0	8 255	0	0	0
China, Macao SAR	1	10	1	159	0	0
Christmas Island	0	0	0	1	0	0
Cocos (Keeling) Islands	0	0	0	0	0	0
Colombia	0[e]	2[f]	2 912[g]	P	0	0
Cook Islands	0	0	0	1	0	0
Costa Rica	0	0	676	29	0	0
Côte d'Ivoire	30	1	25	500	0	0
Croatia	30	0	0	0	0	0
Cuba	200			6	0[c]	

Country or territory	Ephedrine	Ephedrine preparations	Pseudoephedrine	Pseudoephedrine preparations	3,4-MDP-2-P[a]	P-2-P[b]
Curaçao	0		0		0	0
Cyprus	10	5	500	270	0	0
Czech Republic	26	4	750	390	0	1
Democratic People's Republic of Korea	300	1 200	0	0	5	0
Democratic Republic of the Congo	300	10	720	900	0[c]	
Denmark					0	0
Dominican Republic	75	4	300	175	0	0
Ecuador	10	6	600	2 500	0	0
Egypt	4 500	0	55 000	2 500	0	0
El Salvador	P(6)[h]	P(10)[h]	P	P	0	0
Eritrea	0	0	0	0	0	0
Estonia	5	5	0	500	0	0
Falkland Islands (Malvinas)		1		1	0[c]	
Faroe Islands	0	0	0	0	0	0
Finland	4	60	1	650	0[c]	1
France	3 500	10	20 000	500	0	0
Gambia	0	0	0	0	0	0
Georgia	5	25	2	15	0	0
Germany	1 000		7 000		1	8
Ghana	4 500	300	3 000	200	0	0
Greece	100		3 000		0	0
Greenland	0	0	0	0	0	0
Guatemala	0		P	P	0	0
Guinea	36				0[c]	
Guinea-Bissau	0	0	0	0	0	0
Guyana	120	50	120	30	0	0
Haiti	200	1	350	12	0	0
Honduras	P	P(1)[f]	P	P	0	0
Hungary	650		1		0	800
Iceland	0	0	0	0	0	0
India	2 200	112 729	333 585	1 092	0	0
Indonesia	10 500	0	52 000	6 200	0	0
Iran (Islamic Republic of)	2	1	17 000	1	1	1
Iraq	3 000	100	14 000	10 000	0	P[i]
Ireland	1	3	1	1 145	0	0
Israel	25	5	2 913	80	0[c]	
Italy	1 000	0	26 000	18 000	0	250
Jamaica	50	150	400	300	0	0
Japan	1 000		12 000		0[c]	
Jordan	150		10 600		0[c]	P
Kazakhstan	0		0		0	0
Kenya	2 500		3 000		0[c]	

Country or territory	Ephedrine	Ephedrine preparations	Pseudoephedrine	Pseudoephedrine preparations	3,4-MDP-2-P[a]	P-2-P[b]
Kyrgyzstan	0	0	0	100	0	0
Lao People's Democratic Republic	0	0	1 000	130	0	0
Latvia	20	27	65	350	0	0
Lebanon	26	5	240	700	0	0
Lithuania	1	1	1	650	1	1
Luxembourg	1	0	0	0	0	0
Madagascar	702	180	150		0[c]	
Malawi	1 000				0[c]	
Malaysia	20	15	4 536	3 169	0	0
Maldives	0	0	0	0	0	0
Malta		220	220	220	0	0
Mauritius	0	0	0	0	0	0
Mexico	P(500)[h]	P[h]	P	P	0	0
Monaco	0	0	0	0	0	0
Mongolia	3				0[c]	
Montenegro	0	1	0	100	0	0
Montserrat	0	1	0	1	0	0
Morocco	41	14	2 642	0	0	0
Mozambique	3				0[c]	
Myanmar	2	11	0	0	0	0
Namibia	0	0	0	0	0	0
Nepal		1	5 000		0[c]	
Netherlands	200	1 107		43 259	0	0
New Zealand	50	0	800		0	3
Nicaragua	P[i]	P[i]	P	P	0	0
Nigeria	9 650	500	5 823	15 000	0	0
Norfolk Island	0	0	0	0	0	0
Norway	225	0	1	0	0	0
Pakistan	12 000		48 000	500	0[c]	
Panama	6	6	400	500	0	
Papua New Guinea	1		200		0	0
Paraguay	0	0	2 500	0	0	0
Peru	54		2 524	1 078	0[c]	
Philippines	72	0	149	0	0	0
Poland	160	0	5 170	0	1	4
Portugal			15		0[c]	
Qatar	0	0	0	80	0	0
Republic of Korea	22 650		44 100		1	1
Republic of Moldova	0	0	0	600	0	0
Romania	197		10 906		0	0
Russian Federation	1 500				0[c]	
Saint Helena	0	1	0	1	0	0

Country or territory	Ephedrine	Ephedrine preparations	Pseudoephedrine	Pseudoephedrine preparations	3,4-MDP-2-P[a]	P-2-P[b]
Saint Lucia	0	0	0	0	0	0
Saint Vincent and the Grenadines	0		0		0	0
Sao Tome and Principe	0	0	0	0	0	0
Saudi Arabia	1	0	20 000	0	0	0
Senegal	82	0	0	304	0	0
Serbia	25	0	1 265	0	0	1
Singapore	10 565	5	35 000	1 700	1	1
Slovakia	4	6	1	1	0	0
Slovenia	9		250		0	0
Solomon Islands	0	1	0	1	0	0
South Africa	13 900	0	10 444	10 816	0	0
Spain	205		4 956		0	111
Sri Lanka		0		0	0	0
Sweden	193	165	1	1	1	13
Switzerland	3 100		85 000		1	500
Syrian Arab Republic	1 000		50 000		0[c]	
Tajikistan	38				0[c]	
Thailand	53	0	1	0	0[c]	0
Trinidad and Tobago					0[c]	0
Tristan da Cunha	0	0	0	0	0	0
Tunisia	1	18	4 000	0	0	30
Turkey	250	0	22 000	4 000	0	0
Turkmenistan	0	0	0	0	0	0
Uganda	150	35	2 500	400	0	0
Ukraine	0	81	0	3 247	0	0
United Arab Emirates	0		3 000	2 499	0	0
United Kingdom	64 448	1 011	25 460	1 683	8	1
United Republic of Tanzania	100	1 500	2 000	100	0[c]	
United States of America	5 000		224 507		0	34 375
Uruguay	0	0	1	0	0	0
Uzbekistan	0	0	0		0	0
Venezuela (Bolivarian Republic of)	60	1 000	3 060	2 000	0	0
Yemen	75	75	3 000	2 000	0[c]	
Zambia	50	25	50	100	0[c]	
Zimbabwe	150	150	150	50	1 000	1 000

Notes: The names of territories, departments and special administrative regions are in italics.

A blank field signifies that no requirement was indicated or that data were not submitted for the substance in question.

A zero (0) signifies that the country or territory currently has no licit requirement for the substance.

The letter "P" signifies that importation of the substance is prohibited.

Reported quantities of less than 1 kg have been rounded up and are reflected as 1 kg.

[a] 3,4-Methylenedioxyphenyl-2-propanone.

[b] 1-Phenyl-2-propanone.

^c The Board is currently unaware of any legitimate need for the importation of this substance into the country.

^d Including the licit requirements for pharmaceutical preparations containing the substance.

^e The required amount of ephedrine is to be used for the manufacture of injectable ephedrine sulphate solution.

^f In the form of injectable ephedrine sulphate solution.

^g The required amount of pseudoephedrine is to be used exclusively for the manufacture of medicines for export.

^h Imports of the substance and preparations containing the substance are prohibited, with the exception of the imports of injectable ephedrine preparations and ephedrine as a prime raw material for the manufacture of such ephedrine preparations. Pre-export notification is required for each individual import.

ⁱ Includes products containing P-2-P.

^j Imports of the substance and preparations containing the substance are prohibited, with the exception of the imports of injectable ephedrine preparations and ephedrine as a prime raw material for the manufacture of such ephedrine preparations. Such export requires an import permit.

Annex III

Substances in Tables I and II of the 1988 Convention

Table I	*Table II*
Acetic anhydride	Acetone
N-Acetylanthranilic acid	Anthranilic acid
Ephedrine	Ethyl ether
Ergometrine	Hydrochloric acid[a]
Ergotamine	Methyl ethyl ketone
Isosafrole	Piperidine
Lysergic acid	Sulphuric acid[a]
3,4-Methylenedioxyphenyl-2-propanone	Toluene
Norephedrine	
Phenylacetic acid	
alpha-Phenylacetoacetonitrile[b]	
1-Phenyl-2-propanone	
Piperonal	
Potassium permanganate	
Pseudoephedrine	
Safrole	

The salts of the substances listed in this Table whenever the existence of such salts is possible.

The salts of the substances listed in this Table whenever the existence of such salts is possible.

---

[a] The salts of hydrochloric acid and sulphuric acid are specifically excluded from Table II.
[b] Included in Table I, effective 9 October 2014.

Annex IV

Use of scheduled substances in the illicit manufacture of narcotic drugs and psychotropic substances

Figures A.I-A.IV below depict the use of scheduled substances in the illicit manufacture of narcotic drugs and psychotropic substances. The approximate quantities provided are based on common manufacturing methods. Other manufacturing methods using scheduled substances — or even non-scheduled substances instead of or in addition to scheduled substances — may also be encountered, depending on the geographical location.

Figure A.I. Illicit manufacture of cocaine and heroin: scheduled substances and the approximate quantities thereof required for the illicit manufacture of 100 kilograms of cocaine or heroin hydrochloride

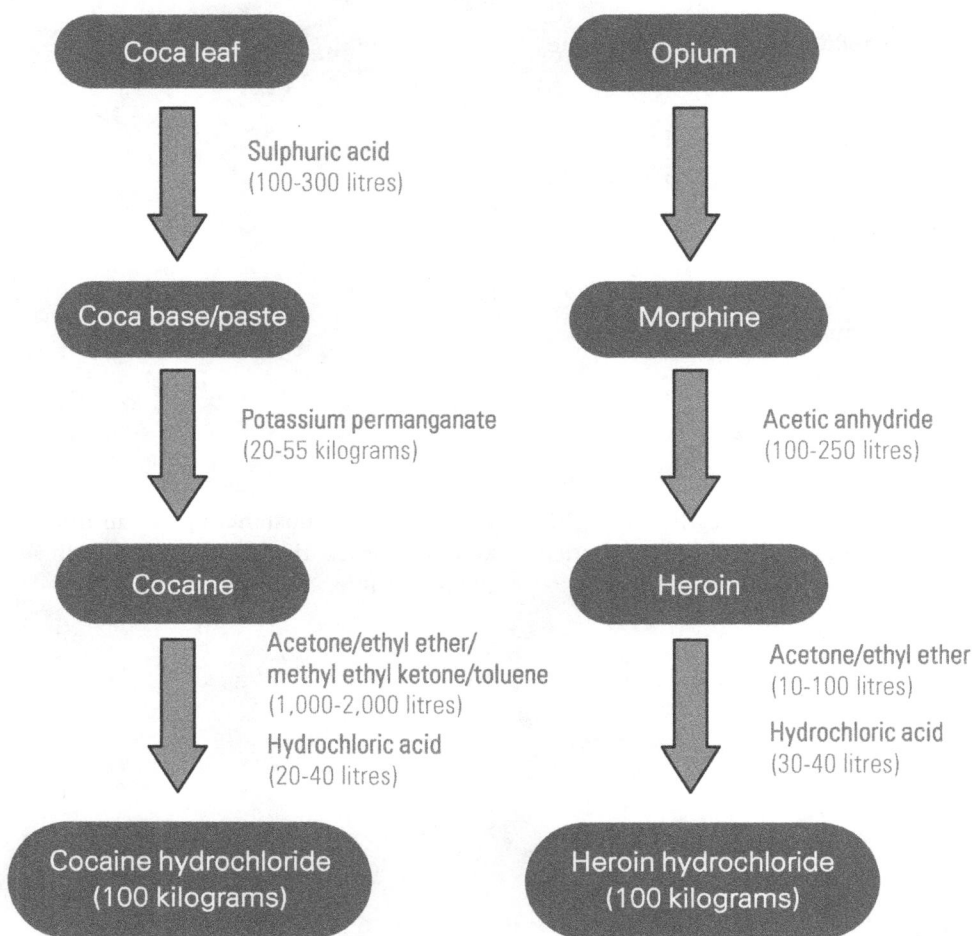

Note: The extraction of cocaine from coca leaf and the purification of coca paste and the crude base products of cocaine and heroin require solvents, acids and bases. A wide range of such chemicals have been used at all stages of drug manufacture.

Figure A.II. Illicit manufacture of amphetamine and methamphetamine: scheduled substances and the approximate quantities thereof required for the illicit manufacture of 100 kilograms of amphetamine sulphate and methamphetamine hydrochloride

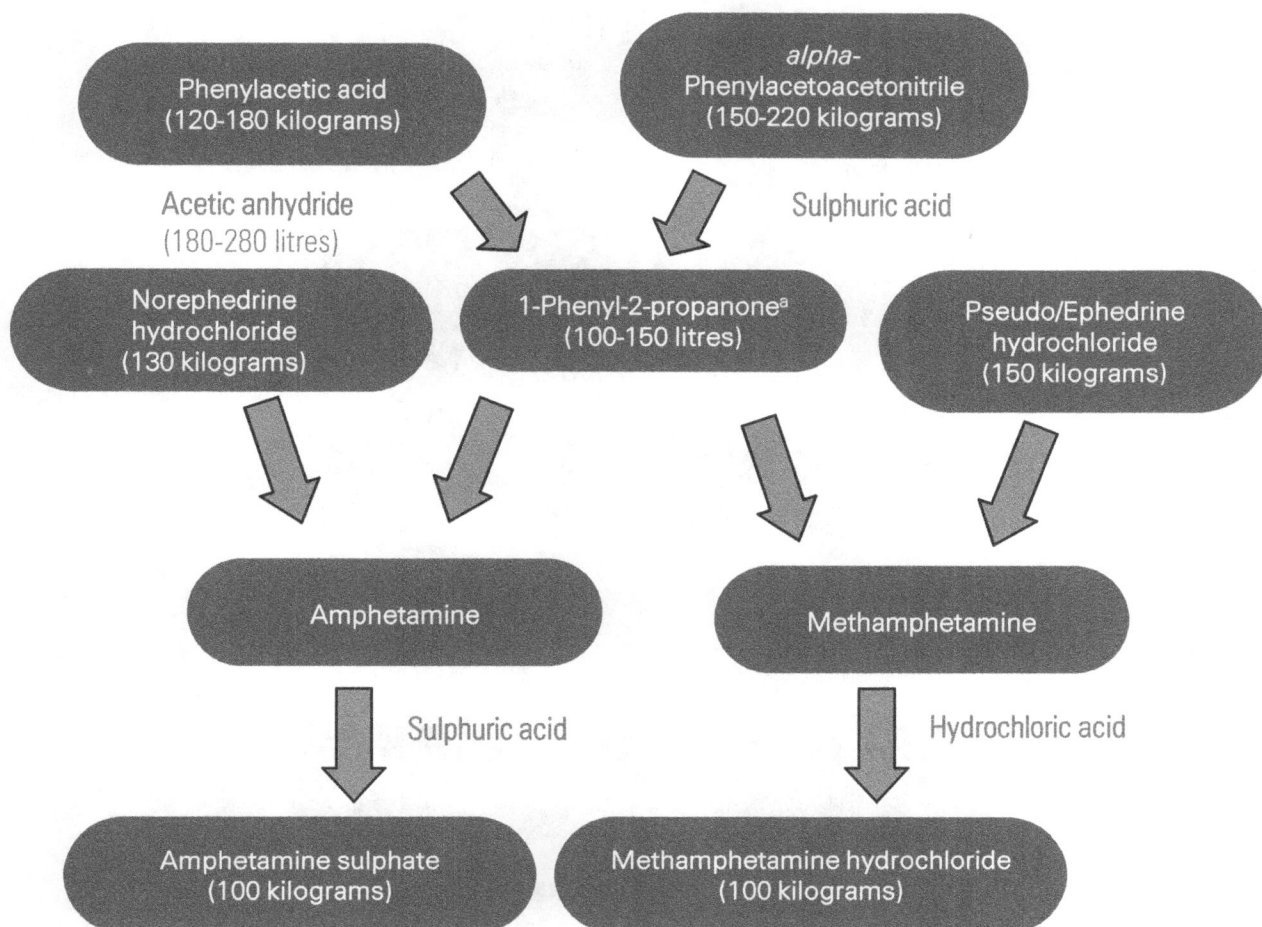

Note: Methcathinone, a less commonly encountered amphetamine-type stimulant, can be manufactured from pseudo/ephedrine hydrochloride, requiring the same approximate quantities as methamphetamine to yield 100 kilograms of hydrochloride salt.

[a] Methods based on 1-phenyl-2-propanone result in racemic *d,l*-meth/amphetamine while methods based on ephedrine, pseudoephedrine or norephedrine result in *d*-meth/amphetamine.

Figure A.III. Illicit manufacture of 3,4-methylenedioxymethamphetamine (MDMA) and related drugs: scheduled substances and the approximate quantities thereof required for the illicit manufacture of 100 kilograms of MDMA

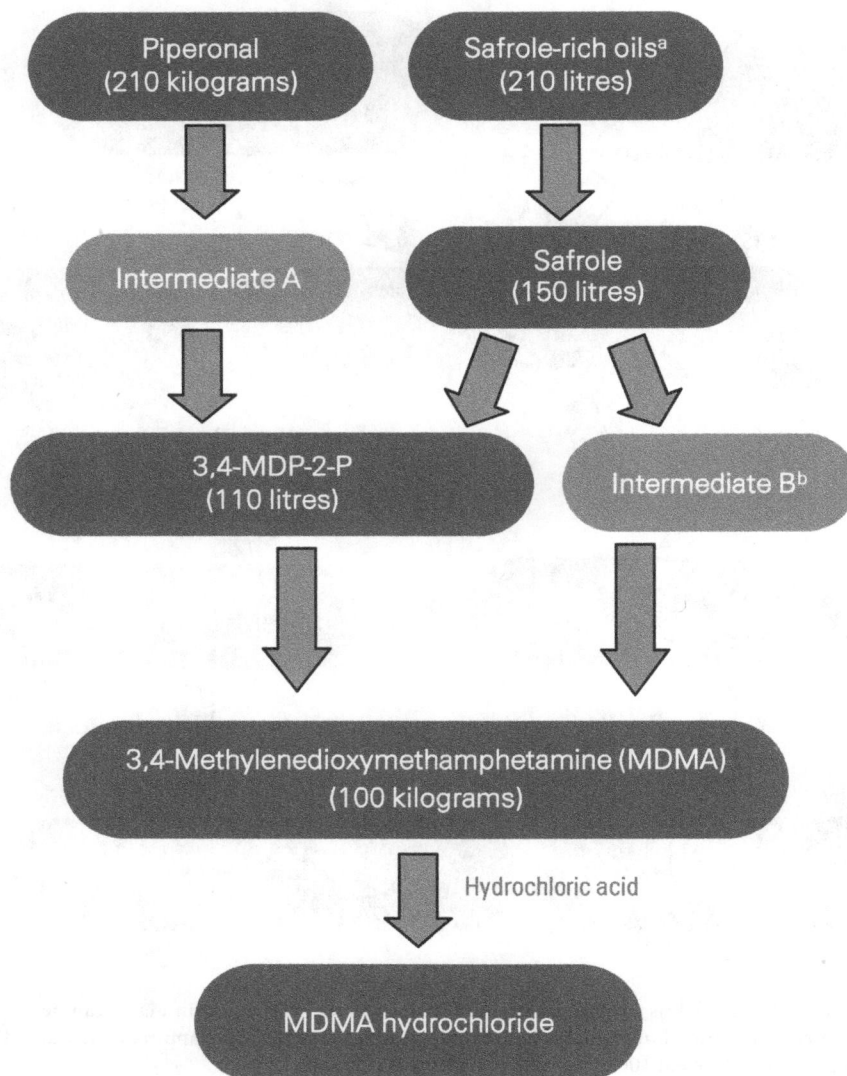

Note: Isosafrole, another precursor of MDMA under international control, is not included in this scheme, as it is not commonly encountered as a starting material; it is an intermediate in a modification of methods for manufacturing MDMA from safrole, requiring approximately 300 litres of safrole to manufacture 100 kilograms of MDMA.

[a] Assuming the safrole-rich oils have a safrole content of 75 per cent or higher.

[b] The manufacture of 100 kilograms of MDMA via intermediate B would require 200 litres of safrole.

Figure A.IV. Illicit manufacture of lysergic acid diethylamide (LSD), methaqualone and phencyclidine: scheduled substances and the approximate quantities thereof required for the illicit manufacture of 1 kilogram of LSD and 100 kilograms of methaqualone and phencyclidine

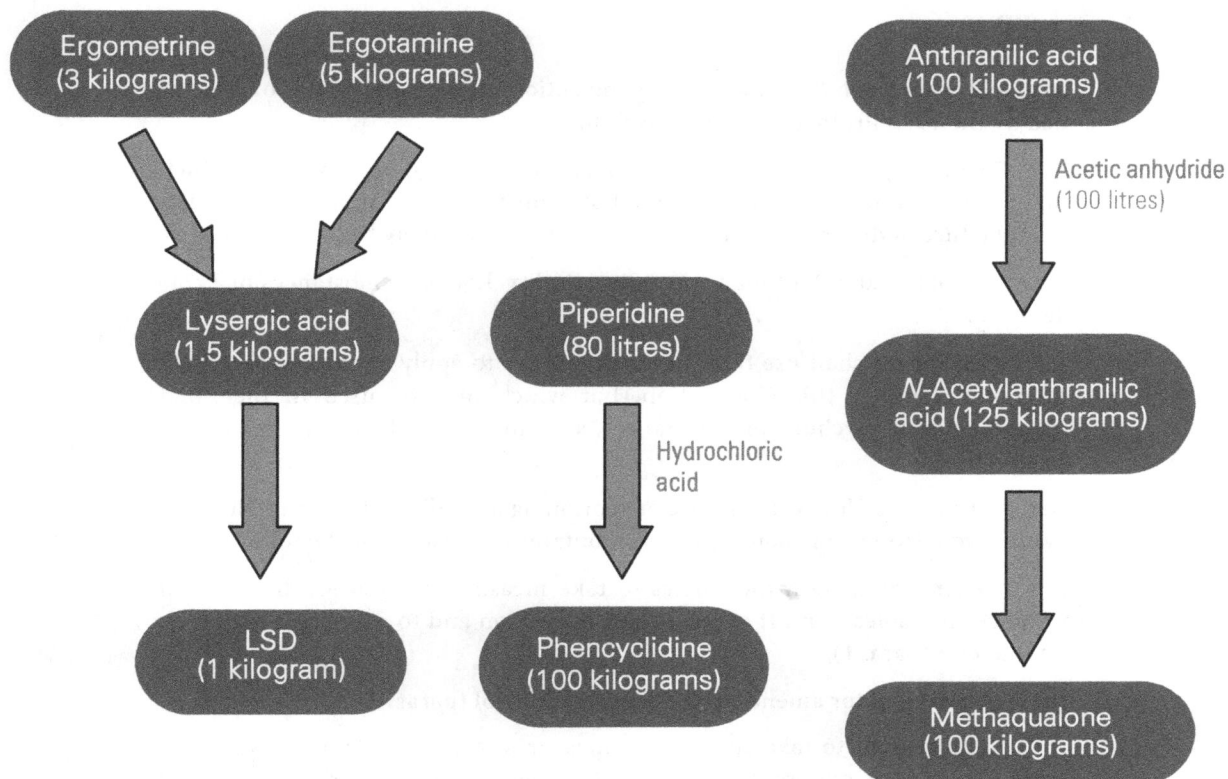

Annex V

Treaty provisions for the control of substances frequently used in the illicit manufacture of narcotic drugs and psychotropic substances

1. Article 2, paragraph 8, of the Single Convention on Narcotic Drugs of 1961 as amended by the 1972 Protocol[a] provides as follows:

> The Parties shall use their best endeavours to apply to substances which do not fall under this Convention, but which may be used in the illicit manufacture of drugs, such measures of supervision as may be practicable.

2. Article 2, paragraph 9, of the Convention on Psychotropic Substances of 1971[b] provides as follows:

> The Parties shall use their best endeavours to apply to substances which do not fall under this Convention, but which may be used in the illicit manufacture of psychotropic substances, such measures of supervision as may be practicable.

3. Article 12 of the United Nations Convention against Illicit Traffic in Narcotic Drugs and Psychotropic Substances of 1988[c] contains provisions for the following:

(a) General obligation for parties to take measures to prevent diversion of the substances in Tables I and II of the 1988 Convention and to cooperate with each other to that end (para. 1);

(b) Mechanism for amending the scope of control (paras. 2-7);

(c) Requirement to take appropriate measures to monitor manufacture and distribution, to which end parties may control persons and enterprises, control establishments and premises under licence, require permits for such operations and prevent accumulation of substances in Tables I and II (para. 8);

(d) Obligation to monitor international trade in order to identify suspicious transactions, to provide for seizures, to notify the authorities of the parties concerned in case of suspicious transactions, to require proper labelling and documentation and to ensure maintenance of such documents for at least two years (para. 9);

(e) Mechanism for advance notice of exports of substances in Table I, upon request (para. 10);

(f) Confidentiality of information (para. 11);

(g) Reporting by parties to the International Narcotics Control Board (para. 12);

(h) Report of the Board to the Commission on Narcotic Drugs (para. 13);

(i) Non-applicability of the provisions of article 12 to certain preparations (para. 14).

---

[a] United Nations, *Treaty Series*, vol. 976, No. 14152.
[b] Ibid., vol. 1019, No. 14956.
[c] Ibid., vol. 1582, No. 27627.

Annex VI

Regional groupings

Reference is made throughout the present report to various geographical regions, which are defined as follows:

Africa: Algeria, Angola, Benin, Botswana, Burkina Faso, Burundi, Cabo Verde, Cameroon, Central African Republic, Chad, Comoros, Congo, Côte d'Ivoire, Democratic Republic of the Congo, Djibouti, Egypt, Equatorial Guinea, Eritrea, Ethiopia, Gabon, Gambia, Ghana, Guinea, Guinea-Bissau, Kenya, Lesotho, Liberia, Libya, Madagascar, Malawi, Mali, Mauritania, Mauritius, Morocco, Mozambique, Namibia, Niger, Nigeria, Rwanda, Sao Tome and Principe, Senegal, Seychelles, Sierra Leone, Somalia, South Africa, South Sudan, Sudan, Swaziland, Togo, Tunisia, Uganda, United Republic of Tanzania, Zambia and Zimbabwe;

Central America and the Caribbean: Antigua and Barbuda, Bahamas, Barbados, Belize, Costa Rica, Cuba, Dominica, Dominican Republic, El Salvador, Grenada, Guatemala, Haiti, Honduras, Jamaica, Nicaragua, Panama, Saint Kitts and Nevis, Saint Lucia, Saint Vincent and the Grenadines and Trinidad and Tobago;

North America: Canada, Mexico and United States of America;

South America: Argentina, Bolivia (Plurinational State of), Brazil, Chile, Colombia, Ecuador, Guyana, Paraguay, Peru, Suriname, Uruguay and Venezuela (Bolivarian Republic of);

East and South-East Asia: Brunei Darussalam, Cambodia, China, Democratic People's Republic of Korea, Indonesia, Japan, Lao People's Democratic Republic, Malaysia, Mongolia, Myanmar, Philippines, Republic of Korea, Singapore, Thailand, Timor-Leste and Viet Nam;

South Asia: Bangladesh, Bhutan, India, Maldives, Nepal and Sri Lanka;

West Asia: Afghanistan, Armenia, Azerbaijan, Bahrain, Georgia, Iran (Islamic Republic of), Iraq, Israel, Jordan, Kazakhstan, Kuwait, Kyrgyzstan, Lebanon, Oman, Pakistan, Qatar, Saudi Arabia, State of Palestine, Syrian Arab Republic, Tajikistan, Turkey, Turkmenistan, United Arab Emirates, Uzbekistan and Yemen;

Europe:

> **Eastern Europe:** Belarus, Republic of Moldova, Russian Federation and Ukraine;
>
> **South-Eastern Europe:** Albania, Bosnia and Herzegovina, Bulgaria, Croatia, Montenegro, Romania, Serbia and the former Yugoslav Republic of Macedonia;
>
> **Western and Central Europe:** Andorra, Austria, Belgium, Cyprus, Czech Republic, Denmark, Estonia, Finland, France, Germany, Greece, Holy See, Hungary, Iceland, Ireland, Italy, Latvia, Liechtenstein, Lithuania, Luxembourg, Malta, Monaco, Netherlands, Norway, Poland, Portugal, San Marino, Slovakia, Slovenia, Spain, Sweden, Switzerland and United Kingdom of Great Britain and Northern Ireland;

Oceania: Australia, Cook Islands, Fiji, Kiribati, Marshall Islands, Micronesia (Federated States of), Nauru, New Zealand, Niue, Palau, Papua New Guinea, Samoa, Solomon Islands, Tonga, Tuvalu and Vanuatu.

Annex VII

Submission of information by Governments pursuant to article 12 of the 1988 Convention (form D) for the years 2010-2014

Notes: The names of non-metropolitan territories and special administrative regions are in italics.

A blank signifies that form D was not received.

"X" signifies that a completed form D (or equivalent report) was submitted, including nil returns.

Entries for parties to the 1988 Convention (and for the years that they have been parties) are shaded.

Country or territory	2010	2011	2012	2013	2014
Afghanistan	X	X	X	X	X
Albania	X	X	X	X	X
Algeria	X	X	X	X	X
Andorra	X	X	X	X	X
Angola					
Anguilla[a]				X	
Antigua and Barbuda					
Argentina	X	X	X	X	X
Armenia	X	X	X	X	X
Aruba[a]					
Ascension Island	X	X	X		
Australia	X	X	X	X	X
Austria[b]	X	X	X	X	X
Azerbaijan	X	X	X	X	X
Bahamas					
Bahrain	X				
Bangladesh	X	X	X	X	X
Barbados				X	
Belarus	X	X	X	X	X
Belgium[b]	X	X	X	X	X
Belize				X	
Benin	X	X	X		X
Bermuda[a]					
Bhutan	X	X	X		X
Bolivia (Plurinational State of)	X	X	X	X	X
Bosnia and Herzegovina	X	X	X	X	X
Botswana					
Brazil	X	X	X	X	X
British Virgin Islands[a]					
Brunei Darussalam	X	X	X	X	X
Bulgaria	X	X	X	X	X
Burkina Faso		X			
Burundi					
Cabo Verde					
Cambodia	X	X	X	X	X
Cameroon	X	X	X	X	
Canada	X	X	X	X	
Cayman Islands[a]			X	X	X
Central African Republic					
Chad				X	
Chile	X	X	X	X	X
China	X	X	X	X	X
China, Hong Kong SAR	X		X	X	
China, Macao SAR	X		X	X	X

Country or territory	2010	2011	2012	2013	2014
Christmas Island[a]	X	X		X	X
Cocos (Keeling) Islands[a]	X	X		X	X
Colombia	X	X	X	X	X
Comoros					
Congo					
Cook Islands	X	X			
Costa Rica	X	X	X	X	X
Côte d'Ivoire	X	X	X	X	X
Croatia[b]	X	X	X	X	X
Cuba	X	X			
Curaçao[c]	X	X	X	X	X
Cyprus[b]	X	X	X	X	X
Czech Republic[b]	X	X	X	X	X
Democratic People's Republic of Korea	X	X	X	X	
Democratic Republic of the Congo	X	X	X	X	X
Denmark[b]	X	X	X	X	X
Djibouti					
Dominica					
Dominican Republic	X			X	X
Ecuador	X	X	X	X	X
Egypt	X	X	X	X	X
El Salvador	X	X	X	X	X
Equatorial Guinea					
Eritrea	X	X	X		
Estonia[b]	X	X	X	X	X
Ethiopia		X	X	X	
Falkland Islands (Malvinas)	X	X	X	X	X
Fiji		X			
Finland[b]	X	X	X	X	X
France[b]	X	X	X	X	X
French Polynesia[a]					
Gabon					
Gambia	X	X		X	
Georgia	X	X	X	X	X
Germany[b]	X	X	X	X	X
Ghana	X	X	X	X	X
Gibraltar					
Greece[b]	X	X	X	X	X
Grenada					
Guatemala	X	X	X	X	X
Guinea					
Guinea-Bissau			X		
Guyana	X				X
Haiti	X	X		X	
Holy See					
Honduras		X	X	X	
Hungary[b]	X	X	X	X	X
Iceland	X	X	X	X	X
India	X	X	X	X	
Indonesia	X	X	X	X	X
Iran (Islamic Republic of)	X			X	X
Iraq	X	X			
Ireland[b]	X	X	X	X	X
Israel	X	X	X	X	X
Italy[b]	X	X	X	X	X

Country or territory	2010	2011	2012	2013	2014
Jamaica	X			X	X
Japan	X	X	X	X	X
Jordan	X	X	X	X	X
Kazakhstan	X	X	X	X	
Kenya	X				
Kiribati					
Kuwait			X	X	
Kyrgyzstan	X	X	X	X	X
Lao People's Democratic Republic	X	X	X	X	X
Latvia[b]	X	X	X	X	X
Lebanon	X	X	X	X	X
Lesotho					
Liberia					
Libya					
Liechtenstein					
Lithuania[b]	X	X	X	X	X
Luxembourg[b]	X	X	X	X	X
Madagascar	X			X	
Malawi					
Malaysia	X	X	X	X	X
Maldives	X	X	X	X	
Mali				X	
Malta[b]	X	X	X	X	X
Marshall Islands					
Mauritania					
Mauritius	X	X	X		
Mexico	X	X	X	X	X
Micronesia (Federated States of)				X	
Monaco					
Mongolia			X		
Montenegro	X	X	X	X	X
Montserrat[a]	X		X	X	X
Morocco	X	X	X	X	
Mozambique	X				X
Myanmar	X	X	X	X	X
Namibia	X				X
Nauru					
Nepal				X	X
Netherlands[b]	X	X	X	X	X
New Caledonia[a]	X	X	X	X	X
New Zealand	X	X	X	X	
Nicaragua	X	X	X	X	X
Niger					
Nigeria		X	X	X	
Niue					
Norfolk Island[d]	X	X		X	X
Norway	X		X		
Oman					X
Pakistan	X	X	X	X	X
Palau				X	
Panama	X	X	X	X	X
Papua New Guinea					
Paraguay	X	X		X	
Peru	X	X	X	X	X
Philippines	X	X	X	X	X

Country or territory	2010	2011	2012	2013	2014
Poland[b]	X	X	X	X	X
Portugal[b]	X	X	X	X	X
Qatar		X		X	
Republic of Korea	X	X	X	X	X
Republic of Moldova	X	X	X	X	X
Romania[b]	X	X	X	X	X
Russian Federation	X	X	X	X	X
Rwanda					
Saint Helena		X			
Saint Kitts and Nevis					
Saint Lucia	X	X	X	X	X
Saint Vincent and the Grenadines			X	X	X
Samoa	X	X	X		
San Marino					
Sao Tome and Principe		X			
Saudi Arabia	X	X	X	X	X
Senegal	X			X	X
Serbia	X	X	X	X	
Seychelles		X	X		
Sierra Leone					
Singapore	X	X	X	X	X
Sint Maarten[c]					
Slovakia[b]	X	X	X	X	X
Slovenia[b]	X	X	X	X	X
Solomon Islands					
Somalia					
South Africa				X	
South Sudan[e]					
Spain[b]	X	X	X	X	X
Sri Lanka	X	X	X	X	X
Sudan					X
Suriname					
Swaziland					
Sweden[b]	X	X	X	X	X
Switzerland	X	X	X	X	X
Syrian Arab Republic	X		X	X	
Tajikistan	X	X	X	X	
Thailand	X	X	X	X	X
The former Yugoslav Republic of Macedonia	X				
Timor-Leste					
Togo			X		
Tonga					
Trinidad and Tobago	X	X	X	X	X
Tristan da Cunha					
Tunisia	X	X	X	X	X
Turkey	X	X	X	X	X
Turkmenistan		X	X	X	X
Turks and Caicos Islands[a]					
Tuvalu		X	X		
Uganda	X	X	X	X	X
Ukraine	X	X	X	X	
United Arab Emirates	X	X	X	X	X
United Kingdom[b]	X	X	X	X	X
United Republic of Tanzania	X	X	X	X	X
United States of America	X	X	X	X	X

Country or territory	2010	2011	2012	2013	2014
Uruguay	X	X	X	X	X
Uzbekistan	X	X	X	X	X
Vanuatu		X			
Venezuela (Bolivarian Republic of)	X	X	X	X	X
Viet Nam	X	X	X	X	X
Wallis and Futuna Islands[a]					
Yemen	X	X	X		
Zambia					X
Zimbabwe	X			X	X
Total number of Governments that submitted form D[f]	**139**	**134**	**130**	**139**	**117**
Total number of Governments requested to provide information	**213**	**213**	**213**	**213**	**213**

[a] Territorial application of the 1988 Convention has been confirmed by the authorities concerned.

[b] State member of the European Union.

[c] The Netherlands Antilles was dissolved on 10 October 2010, resulting in two new constituent entities, Curaçao and Sint Maarten. The authorities of Curaçao submitted form D for 2010 for the former Netherlands Antilles.

[d] Information was provided by Australia.

[e] By its resolution 65/308 of 14 July 2011, the General Assembly decided to admit South Sudan to membership in the United Nations.

[f] In addition, the European Commission submitted form D for the years 2010-2014.

Annex VIII

Seizures of substances in Tables I and II of the 1988 Convention, as reported to the International Narcotics Control Board, 2010-2014

1.   Tables A.1 and A.2 below show information on seizures of the substances included in Tables I and II of the United Nations Convention against Illicit Traffic in Narcotic Drugs and Psychotropic Substances of 1988, furnished to the International Narcotics Control Board by Governments in accordance with article 12, paragraph 12, of the Convention.

2.   The tables include data on domestic seizures and on seizures effected at points of entry or exit. They do not include reported seizures of substances where it is known that the substances were not intended for the illicit manufacture of drugs (for example, seizures effected on administrative grounds or seizures of ephedrine/pseudoephedrine preparations to be used as stimulants). Stopped shipments are also not included. The information may include data submitted by Governments through means other than form D; in such cases, the sources are duly noted.

Units of measure and conversion factors

3.   Units of measure are indicated for every substance. As fractions of full units are not listed in the tables, figures are rounded as necessary.

4.   For a variety of reasons, individual quantities of some substances seized are reported to the Board using different units; for instance, one country may report seizures of acetic anhydride in litres, another in kilograms.

5.   To enable a proper comparison of collected information, it is important that all data be collated in a standard format. To simplify the necessary standardization process, figures are given in grams or kilograms where the substance is a solid and in litres where the substance (or its most common form) is a liquid.

6.   Seizures of solids reported to the Board in litres have not been converted into kilograms and are not included in the tables, as the actual quantity of substance in solution is not known.

7.   For seizures of liquids, quantities reported in kilograms have been converted into litres using the following factors:

Substance	Conversion factor (kilograms to litres)[a]
Acetic anhydride	0.926
Acetone	1.269
Ethyl ether	1.408
Hydrochloric acid (39.1% solution)	0.833
Isosafrole	0.892
3,4-Methylenedioxyphenyl-2-propanone	0.833
Methyl ethyl ketone	1.242
1-Phenyl-2-propanone	0.985
Piperidine	1.160
Safrole	0.912
Sulphuric acid (concentrated solution)	0.543
Toluene	1.155

[a] Derived from density (*The Merck Index* (Rahway, New Jersey, Merck, 1989)).

8.   As an example, to convert 1,000 kilograms of methyl ethyl ketone into litres, multiply by 1.242, i.e. 1,000 × 1.242 = 1,242 litres.

9.   For the conversion of gallons to litres, it has been assumed that in Colombia the United States gallon is used, with 3.785 litres to the gallon, and in Myanmar the imperial gallon is used, with 4.546 litres to the gallon.

10.   If reported quantities have been converted, the converted figures are listed in the tables in italics.

11.   The names of territories appear in italics.

12.   A dash (–) signifies that the report did not include data on seizures of the particular substance in the reporting year.

13.   A degree symbol (°) signifies less than the smallest unit of measurement shown for that substance (for example, less than 1 kilogram).

14.   Discrepancies may exist between the regional total seizure figures and the world total figures because the actual quantities seized were rounded to whole numbers.

Table A.1. Seizures of substances in Table I of the 1988 Convention as reported to the International Narcotics Control Board, 2010-2014

Country or territory, by region / Year	Acetic anhydride (litres)	N-Acetylanthranilic acid (kilograms)	Ephedrine (kilograms)	Ephedrine preparations[a] (kilograms)	Ergometrine (grams)	Ergotamine (grams)	Isosafrole (litres)	Lysergic acid (grams)	3,4-Methylenedioxyphenyl-2-propanone (litres)	1-Phenyl-2-propanone (litres)	Norephedrine (phenylpropanolamine) (kilograms)	Phenylacetic acid (kilograms)	alpha-phenylacetoacetonitrile[b] (kilograms)	Piperonal (kilograms)	Potassium permanganate (kilograms)	Pseudoephedrine (kilograms)	Pseudoephedrine preparations[a] (kilograms)	Safrole (litres)
Africa																		
Côte d'Ivoire																		
2011	—	—	—	[b]	—	—	—	—	—	—	—	—	—	—	—	—	[b]	—
2012	—	—	—	[b]	—	—	—	—	—	—	—	—	—	—	—	—	—	—
2013	—	—	—	1	—	—	—	—	—	—	—	—	—	—	—	—	—	—
Namibia																		
2014	—	—	21	—	—	—	2 100	—	—	—	—	—	—	—	—	—	—	—
Nigeria																		
2011	—	—	56	—	—	—	—	—	—	—	—	—	—	—	—	—	—	—
2012	—	—	461	—	—	—	—	—	—	—	—	—	—	—	—	—	—	—
United Republic of Tanzania																		
2014	—	—	4	—	—	—	—	—	—	—	—	—	—	—	—	—	—	—
Zambia																		
2014	—	—	—	—	—	—	—	—	—	—	—	—	—	—	—	—	—	—
Zimbabwe																		
2013	—	—	—	113	—	—	—	—	—	—	—	—	—	—	—	—	—	—
2014	—	—	70	—	—	—	—	—	—	—	—	—	—	—	—	—	—	—
Regional total																		
2010	0	0	0	0	0	0	0	0	0	0	0	0	0	0	0	0	0	0
2011	0	0	56	0	0	0	0	0	0	0	0	0	0	0	0	0	0	0
2012	0	0	461	0	0	0	0	0	0	0	0	0	0	0	0	0	0	0
2013	0	0	0	114	0	0	0	0	0	0	0	0	0	0	0	0	0	0
2014	0	0	95	0	0	0	2 100	0	0	0	0	0	0	0	0	0	0	0

Americas

Central America and the Caribbean

Country or territory, by region / Year	Acetic anhydride (litres)	N-Acetylanthranilic acid (kilograms)	Ephedrine (kilograms)	Ephedrine preparations[a] (kilograms)	Ergometrine (grams)	Ergotamine (grams)	Isosafrole (litres)	Lysergic acid (grams)	3,4-Methylenedioxyphenyl-2-propanone (litres)	1-Phenyl-2-propanone (litres)	Norephedrine (phenylpropanolamine) (kilograms)	Phenylacetic acid (kilograms)	alpha-phenylacetoacetonitrile[b] (kilograms)	Piperonal (kilograms)	Potassium permanganate (kilograms)	Pseudoephedrine (kilograms)	Pseudoephedrine preparations[a] (kilograms)	Safrole (litres)
Belize 2013	660	–	–	–	–	–	–	–	–	–	–	–	–	–	–	–	–	–
Costa Rica 2010	–	–	–	–	–	–	–	–	–	–	–	–	–	–	–	14	–	–
El Salvador 2010	–	–	10	–	–	–	–	–	–	–	–	–	–	–	–	–	–	–
2011	–	–	–	–	–	–	–	–	–	–	–	–	–	–	–	–	○	–
Guatemala 2010	–	–	15	–	–	–	–	–	–	–	–	–	–	–	–	989	–	–
2011	512	–	100	–	–	–	–	–	–	–	–	1	–	–	–	95	–	–
Honduras 2011	–	–	–	–	–	–	–	–	–	–	–	–	–	–	–	–	41	–
2012	–	–	–	–	–	–	–	–	–	–	–	–	–	–	–	22 565	–	–
2013	–	–	–	–	–	–	–	–	–	–	–	–	–	–	–	1	–	–
Nicaragua 2012	–	–	–	–	–	–	–	–	13	–	–	52	–	–	–	–	–	–
Panama 2013	–	–	–	–	–	–	–	–	–	–	22	–	–	–	–	–	–	–
Regional total 2010	0	0	25	0	0	0	0	0	0	0	0	0	0	0	0	1 003	0	0
2011	512	0	100	0	0	0	0	0	0	0	0	1	0	0	0	95	42	0
2012	0	0	0	0	0	0	0	0	13	0	0	52	0	0	0	22 565	0	0
2013	660	0	0	0	0	0	0	0	0	0	22	0	0	0	0	1	0	0
2014	0	0	0	0	0	0	0	0	0	0	0	0	0	0	0	0	0	0

Country or territory, by region	Year	Acetic anhydride (litres)	N-Acetylanthranilic acid (kilograms)	Ephedrine (kilograms)	Ephedrine preparations[a] (kilograms)	Ergometrine (grams)	Ergotamine (grams)	Isosafrole (litres)	Lysergic acid (grams)	3,4-Methylenedioxyphenyl-2-propanone (litres)	1-Phenyl-2-propanone (litres)	Norephedrine (phenylpropanolamine) (kilograms)	Phenylacetic acid (kilograms)	alpha-phenylacetoacetonitrile[b] (kilograms)	Piperonal (kilograms)	Potassium permanganate (kilograms)	Pseudoephedrine (kilograms)	Pseudoephedrine preparations[a] (kilograms)	Safrole (litres)
North America																			
Canada	2010	—	—	676	—	—	—	—	—	—	5 924	—		—	—	16	°	—	—
	2011	—	—	13	—	—	—	—	7	122	—	—		—	—	1	11	—	65
	2012	—	—	686	—	—	20	—	°	—	526	—		—	—	5	309	—	2 025
	2013	4	—	—	—	—	—	—	—	—	—	—		—	—	—	2	—	—
Mexico	2010	4 821	—	5 337	—	2 000	—	—	—	—	14 203	25	56 080	—	—	—	3 912	—	—
	2011	76 625	—	2	—	—	—	—	—	—	2 184	—	14 370	—	°	—	313	—	2 371
	2012	35 040	—	—	—	—	1 630	—	—	—	4 699	—	1 188	—	3	35	62	—	—
	2013	7 597	—	—	—	—	—	—	—	—	2 796	—	3 324	—	—	—	7 197	—	—
	2014	13 368	—	—	—	—	—	—	—	—	5 892	—	1 315	—	—	—	—	—	—
United States of America	2010	61 647	—	6 450	—	—	620	°	—	—	114	23	173 578	—	—	24	11 011	°	1
	2011	24 713	—	17 520	33 566	—	820	—	3	—	200	°	997 330	—	—	224	2 502	°	2 281
	2012	859	—	270	—	—	—	—	3	—	—	—	314	—	—	152	241	—	1
	2013	°	—	16	—	—	—	—	—	—	—	—	—	—	—	—	1 029	—	10
	2014	°	—	1	°	—	—	—	—	—	1	—	—	—	—	—	19	1	—
Regional total	**2010**	**66 468**	**0**	**12 464**	**0**	**2 000**	**620**	**°**	**0**	**0**	**20 241**	**48**	**229 658**	**0**	**0**	**40**	**14 923**	**0**	**1**
	2011	**101 339**	**0**	**17 535**	**33 566**	**0**	**820**	**0**	**9**	**122**	**2 384**	**°**	**1 011 700**	**0**	**°**	**225**	**2 827**	**0**	**4 717**
	2012	**35 900**	**0**	**956**	**0**	**0**	**1 650**	**0**	**3**	**0**	**5 225**	**°**	**1 502**	**0**	**3**	**192**	**612**	**0**	**2 026**
	2013	**7 601**	**0**	**16**	**0**	**0**	**0**	**0**	**0**	**0**	**2 796**	**0**	**3 324**	**0**	**0**	**0**	**8 228**	**0**	**10**
	2014	**13 368**	**0**	**1**	**°**	**0**	**0**	**0**	**0**	**0**	**5 893**	**0**	**1 315**	**0**	**0**	**0**	**19**	**1**	**0**
South America																			
Argentina	2011	—	—	—	—	—	—	—	—	—	—	—		—	—	12	250	—	—
	2012	—	—	9	—	—	—	—	—	—	—	—		—	—	2	—	—	—
	2013	—	—	—	1	—	—	—	—	—	—	—		—	—	2	—	—	—
	2014	33	—	24	—	—	—	—	—	—	—	—		—	—	—	—	—	—

65

Country or territory, by region / Year	Acetic anhydride (litres)	N-Acetylanthranilic acid (kilograms)	Ephedrine (kilograms)	Ephedrine preparations[a] (kilograms)	Ergometrine (grams)	Ergotamine (grams)	Isosafrole (litres)	Lysergic acid (grams)	3,4-Methylenedioxyphenyl-2-propanone (litres)	1-Phenyl-2-propanone (litres)	Norephedrine (phenylpropanolamine) (kilograms)	Phenylacetic acid (kilograms)	alpha-phenylacetoacetonitrile[b] (kilograms)	Piperonal (kilograms)	Potassium permanganate (kilograms)	Pseudoephedrine (kilograms)	Pseudoephedrine preparations[a] (kilograms)	Safrole (litres)
Bolivia (Plurinational State of)																		
2011	—	—	○	—	—	—	—	—	—	—	—	—	—	—	9 914	○	○	—
2012	—	—	—	—	—	—	—	—	—	—	—	—	—	—	964	—	—	—
2013	—	—	—	—	—	—	—	—	—	—	—	—	—	—	3 058	—	—	—
2014	—	—	—	—	—	—	—	—	—	—	—	—	—	—	1 492	—	—	—
Brazil																		
2010	—	—	—	—	—	—	—	—	—	—	—	—	—	—	217	—	—	—
2011	53	—	—	—	—	—	—	—	—	—	—	—	—	—	232	—	41	—
2012	1 878	—	—	—	—	—	—	—	—	—	—	—	—	—	278	—	—	—
2013	249	—	—	—	—	—	—	—	—	—	—	—	—	—	14 621	—	—	—
2014	—	—	—	—	—	—	—	—	—	—	—	—	—	—	1	—	—	—
Colombia																		
2010	1 006	—	—	—	—	—	—	—	—	—	—	—	—	—	26 442	—	—	—
2011	—	—	—	—	—	—	—	—	—	—	—	—	—	—	24 044	—	—	—
2012	11	—	—	—	—	—	—	—	—	—	—	—	—	—	55 677	—	—	—
2013	—	—	—	—	—	—	—	—	—	—	—	—	—	—	21 873	—	—	—
2014	—	—	—	—	—	—	—	—	—	—	—	—	—	—	166 291	—	—	—
Ecuador																		
2010	—	—	—	—	—	—	—	—	—	—	—	—	—	—	589	—	—	—
2011	—	—	—	—	—	—	—	—	—	220	—	—	—	—	233	—	—	—
2014	—	—	—	—	—	—	—	—	—	—	—	—	—	—	10	—	—	—
Paraguay																		
2013	—	—	—	—	—	—	—	—	—	—	—	—	—	—	3 705	—	—	—
Peru																		
2010	—	—	—	—	—	—	—	—	—	—	—	—	—	—	517	—	—	—
2011	—	—	—	—	—	—	—	—	—	—	—	—	—	—	1 997	—	—	—
2012	—	—	—	—	—	—	—	—	—	—	—	—	—	—	3 093	—	—	—
2013	1	—	—	—	—	—	—	—	—	—	—	—	—	—	2 787	—	—	—
2014	15	—	—	—	—	—	—	—	—	—	—	—	—	—	2 735	—	—	—

Country or territory, by region	Year	Acetic anhydride (litres)	N-Acetylanthranilic acid (kilograms)	Ephedrine (kilograms)	Ephedrine preparations[a] (kilograms)	Ergometrine (grams)	Ergotamine (grams)	Isosafrole (litres)	Lysergic acid (grams)	3,4-Methylenedioxyphenyl-2-propanone (litres)	1-Phenyl-2-propanone (litres)	Norephedrine (phenylpropanolamine) (kilograms)	Phenylacetic acid (kilograms)	alpha-phenylacetoacetonitrile[b] (kilograms)	Piperonal (kilograms)	Potassium permanganate (kilograms)	Pseudoephedrine (kilograms)	Pseudoephedrine preparations[a] (kilograms)	Safrole (litres)
Venezuela (Bolivarian Republic of)	2010	—	—	—	—	—	78 360	—	—	—	—	—	—	—	—	—	—	—	—
	2011	—	—	—	16	—	—	—	—	—	—	—	—	—	—	100	—	3	—
	2012	—	—	—	—	—	—	—	—	—	—	—	—	—	—	2 447	—	—	—
	2014	—	—	—	—	—	—	—	—	—	—	—	—	—	—	1 120	—	—	—
Regional total	**2010**	**1 006**	**0**	**0**	**0**	**0**	**78 360**	**0**	**0**	**0**	**0**	**0**	**0**	**0**	**0**	**27 766**	**0**	**0**	**0**
	2011	**53**	**0**	**°**	**16**	**0**	**0**	**0**	**0**	**0**	**220**	**0**	**0**	**0**	**0**	**36 532**	**250**	**44**	**0**
	2012	**1 890**	**0**	**9**	**0**	**0**	**0**	**0**	**0**	**0**	**0**	**0**	**0**	**0**	**0**	**62 462**	**0**	**0**	**0**
	2013	**250**	**0**	**0**	**1**	**0**	**0**	**0**	**0**	**0**	**0**	**0**	**0**	**0**	**0**	**46 046**	**0**	**0**	**0**
	2014	**48**	**0**	**24**	**0**	**0**	**0**	**0**	**0**	**0**	**0**	**0**	**0**	**0**	**0**	**171 649**	**0**	**0**	**0**

Asia

East and South-East Asia

Country or territory, by region	Year	Acetic anhydride (litres)	N-Acetylanthranilic acid (kilograms)	Ephedrine (kilograms)	Ephedrine preparations[a] (kilograms)	Ergometrine (grams)	Ergotamine (grams)	Isosafrole (litres)	Lysergic acid (grams)	3,4-Methylenedioxyphenyl-2-propanone (litres)	1-Phenyl-2-propanone (litres)	Norephedrine (phenylpropanolamine) (kilograms)	Phenylacetic acid (kilograms)	alpha-phenylacetoacetonitrile[b] (kilograms)	Piperonal (kilograms)	Potassium permanganate (kilograms)	Pseudoephedrine (kilograms)	Pseudoephedrine preparations[a] (kilograms)	Safrole (litres)
Cambodia	2011	—	—	3	—	—	—	—	—	—	—	—	—	—	—	—	6	—	2 058
China[d]	2010	16 346	—	4 310	—	—	—	—	—	—	—	—	4 670	—	—	—	1 270	—	—
	2011	16 946	—	4 210	—	—	—	—	—	—	—	—	4 520	—	—	—	1 170	—	—
	2012	17 131	—	3 210	2 428	—	—	—	—	—	259	—	30	—	—	29 927	—	902	—
	2013	94 948	—	11 103	5 718	—	449	—	—	18	5 434	—	6 552	—	—	3 521	908	—	—
	2014	22 635	—	31 576	3 222	—	—	—	—	33	3 241	°	49 651	—	—	2 120	—	—	—
China, Hong Kong SAR	2010	—	—	—	—	—	—	—	—	—	660	—	—	—	—	—	°	—	—
	2012	—	—	—	—	—	—	—	—	—	—	°	—	—	—	—	33	—	—
	2013	—	—	41	—	—	—	—	—	—	—	—	—	—	—	—	34	27	—
China, Macao SAR	2012	—	—	—	167	—	—	—	—	—	—	—	—	—	—	—	—	—	—
Indonesia	2011	—	—	—	—[a]	—	—	—	—	—	—	—	—	—	—	—	—	40	—
	2012	—	—	4	—[a]	—	—	—	—	—	—	4	—	—	—	—	—	—	—

Country or territory, by region / Year	Acetic anhydride (litres)	N-Acetylanthranilic acid (kilograms)	Ephedrine (kilograms)	Ephedrine preparations[a] (kilograms)	Ergometrine (grams)	Ergotamine (grams)	Isosafrole (litres)	Lysergic acid (grams)	3,4-Methylenedioxyphenyl-2-propanone (litres)	1-Phenyl-2-propanone (litres)	Norephedrine (phenylpropanolamine) (kilograms)	Phenylacetic acid (kilograms)	alpha-phenylacetoacetonitrile[b] (kilograms)	Piperonal (kilograms)	Potassium permanganate (kilograms)	Pseudoephedrine (kilograms)	Pseudoephedrine preparations[a] (kilograms)	Safrole (litres)
2013	—	—	°	—	—	—	—	—	—	—	—	—	—	—	—	—	—	257
2014	—	—	°	—ᵃ	—	—	—	—	—	—	—	—	—	—	—	—	—	—
Japan																		
2010	—	—	—	—	—	—	—	—	—	—	2	—	—	—	—	—	—	—
2013	—	—	—	1	—	—	—	—	—	—	—	—	—	—	—	—	—	—
2014	—	—	5	—	—	—	—	—	—	—	—	—	—	—	—	—	—	—
Lao People's Democratic Republic																		
2013	—	—	—	3	—	—	—	—	—	—	—	—	—	—	—	—	—	—
Malaysia																		
2010	—	13	—	—	—	—	—	—	—	—	—	—	—	—	—	5	—	—
2011	—	—	109	91	—	—	—	—	—	—	—	—	—	—	—	903	—	7 675
2012	—	—	—	90	—	—	—	—	—	—	—	—	—	—	—	5	—	—
2013	—	—	66	33	—	—	—	—	—	—	—	—	—	—	—	—	63	—
2014	—	—	—	—	—	—	—	—	—	—	—	—	—	1	—	287	112	—
Myanmar																		
2010	14	—	—	33	—	—	—	—	—	—	—	95	—	—	—	—	766	—
2013	—	—	—	133	—	—	—	—	—	4 800	—	—	—	—	—	—	3 581	—
2014	—	—	—	—	—	—	—	—	—	—	—	—	—	—	—	—	—	—
Philippines																		
2010	—	—	°	—	—	—	—	—	—	—	—	—	—	—	—	°	—	—
2011	—	—	106	—	—	—	—	—	—	—	—	—	—	—	—	—	—	—
2012	—	—	378	—	—	—	—	—	212	—	273	—	—	1	—	3	—	—
2013	—	—	1	—	—	—	—	—	—	—	°	—	—	°	—	609	—	—
2014	—	—	510	—	—	—	—	—	—	—	—	—	—	—	—	—	—	—
Singapore																		
2011	—	—	—	—	—	—	—	—	—	—	—	—	—	—	—	—	155	—
Thailand																		
2010	—	—	3	—	—	—	—	—	—	—	—	—	—	—	—	—	—	—
2011	—	—	3	°	—	—	—	—	—	—	—	—	—	—	·ᵃ	—	1	—

Country or territory, by region / Year	Acetic anhydride (litres)	N-Acetylanthranilic acid (kilograms)	Ephedrine (kilograms)	Ephedrine preparations[a] (kilograms)	Ergometrine (grams)	Ergotamine (grams)	Isosafrole (litres)	Lysergic acid (grams)	3,4-Methylenedioxyphenyl-2-propanone (litres)	1-Phenyl-2-propanone (litres)	Norephedrine (phenylpropanolamine) (kilograms)	Phenylacetic acid (kilograms)	alpha-phenylacetoacetonitrile[b] (kilograms)	Piperonal (kilograms)	Potassium permanganate (kilograms)	Pseudoephedrine (kilograms)	Pseudoephedrine preparations[a] (kilograms)	Safrole (litres)
2012	—	—	17	—	—	—	—	—	—	—	—	—	—	—	—	—	6	—
2014	—	—	—	—	—	—	—	—	—	—	—	—	—	—	—	—	—	—
Viet Nam																		
2013	—	—	—	5	—	—	—	—	—	—	—	—	—	—	—	—	47	—
2014	—	—	4	—	—	—	—	—	—	—	—	—	—	—	—	—	—	—
Regional total																		
2010	**16 360**	**13**	**4 313**	**33**	**0**	**0**	**0**	**0**	**0**	**660**	**2**	**4 670**	**0**	**0**	**0**	**1 275**	**766**	**0**
2011	**16 946**	**0**	**4 431**	**°**	**0**	**0**	**0**	**0**	**0**	**0**	**0**	**4 520**	**0**	**0**	**0**	**2 079**	**196**	**9 734**
2012	**17 131**	**0**	**3 608**	**2 686**	**0**	**0**	**0**	**0**	**212**	**259**	**276**	**30**	**0**	**1**	**29 927**	**40**	**902**	**0**
2013	**94 948**	**0**	**11 211**	**5 950**	**0**	**449**	**0**	**0**	**18**	**5 434**	**°**	**6 647**	**0**	**°**	**3 521**	**1 551**	**3 718**	**257**
2014	**22 635**	**0**	**32 095**	**3 255**	**0**	**0**	**0**	**0**	**33**	**8 041**	**°**	**49 651**	**0**		**2 121**	**309**	**118**	**0**
South Asia																		
India																		
2010	81	—	1 848	—	—	—	—	—	—	—	—	—	—	—	—	359	—	—
2011	—	—	6 308	104	—	—	—	62	—	—	—	—	—	—	—	118	676	—
2012	336	—	559	—	—	—	—	—	—	—	8	—	—	—	—	5 691	236	—
2013	242	—	707	—	—	—	—	—	—	—	—	°	—	—	—	5 098	—	—
Regional total																		
2010	**81**	**0**	**1 848**	**0**	**0**	**0**	**0**	**0**	**0**	**0**	**0**	**0**	**0**	**0**	**0**	**359**	**0**	**0**
2011	**0**	**0**	**6 308**	**104**	**0**	**0**	**0**	**62**	**0**	**0**	**0**	**0**	**0**	**0**	**0**	**118**	**676**	**0**
2012	**336**	**0**	**559**	**0**	**0**	**0**	**0**	**0**	**0**	**0**	**8**	**0**	**0**	**0**	**0**	**5 691**	**236**	**0**
2013	**242**	**0**	**707**	**0**	**0**	**0**	**0**	**0**	**0**	**0**	**0**	**0**	**0**	**0**	**0**	**5 098**	**0**	**0**
2014	**0**	**0**	**0**	**0**	**0**	**0**	**0**	**0**	**0**	**0**	**0**	**0**	**0**	**0**	**0**	**0**	**0**	**0**
West Asia																		
Afghanistan																		
2010	23 260	—	—	—	—	—	—	—	—	—	—	—	—	—	—	—	—	—
2011	68 245	—	—	—	—	—	—	—	—	—	—	—	—	—	—	—	—	—
2012	31 451	—	—	—	—	—	—	—	—	—	—	—	—	—	—	—	—	—
2013	14 212	—	—	—	—	—	—	—	—	—	—	—	—	—	—	—	—	—
2014	7 751	—	—	—	—	—	—	—	—	—	—	—	—	—	—	—	—	—

Country or territory, by region	Year	Acetic anhydride (litres)	N-Acetylanthranilic acid (kilograms)	Ephedrine (kilograms)	Ephedrine preparations[a] (kilograms)	Ergometrine (grams)	Ergotamine (grams)	Isosafrole (litres)	Lysergic acid (grams)	3,4-Methylenedioxyphenyl-2-propanone (litres)	1-Phenyl-2-propanone (litres)	Norephedrine (phenylpropanolamine) (kilograms)	Phenylacetic acid (kilograms)	alpha-phenylacetoacetonitrile[b] (kilograms)	Piperonal (kilograms)	Potassium permanganate (kilograms)	Pseudoephedrine (kilograms)	Pseudoephedrine preparations[a] (kilograms)	Safrole (litres)
Armenia	2010	17	—	—	—	—	—	—	—	—	—	—	—	—	—	—	—	—	—
	2011	1	—	—	—	—	—	—	—	—	—	—	—	—	—	—	—	—	—
	2012	—	—	—	—	—	—	—	—	—	—	—	—	—	—	—	—	—	—
	2013	—	—	—	—	—	—	—	—	—	—	—	—	—	—	—	—	—	—
	2014	—	—	—	—	—	—	—	—	—	—	—	—	—	—	—	—	—	—
Iran (Islamic Republic of)	2010	—	—	2 738[e]	—	—	—	—	—	—	—	—	—	—	—	—	—	—	—
	2011	—	—	3 809[e]	—	—	—	—	—	—	—	—	—	—	—	—	—	—	—
	2013	16 501[e]	—	—	—	—	—	—	—	—	—	—	—	—	—	—	—	—	—
Kazakhstan	2010	1	—	—	—	—	—	—	—	—	—	—	—	—	—	3 285	—	—	—
	2011	—	—	—	—	—	—	—	—	—	—	—	—	—	—	°	—	—	—
	2012	792	—	—	—	—	—	—	—	—	—	—	—	—	—	—	—	—	—
Lebanon	2010	—	—	—	°	—	—	—	—	—	—	—	—	—	—	—	—	—	—
	2012	—	—	6	20	—	—	—	—	—	—	—	—	—	—	—	—	—	—
	2013	—	—	1	—[a]	—	—	—	—	—	—	—	—	—	—	—	—	—	—
	2014	—	—	—	—	—	—	—	—	—	—	—	—	—	—	—	—	—[a]	—
Pakistan	2010	16 178	—	265	—	—	—	—	—	—	—	—	—	—	—	1 250	—	—	—
	2011	43	—	295	—	—	—	—	—	—	—	—	—	—	—	—	—	—	—
	2012	81	—	—	—	—	—	—	—	—	—	—	—	—	—	—	—	—	—
	2013	15 480	—	53	—	—	—	—	—	—	—	—	—	—	—	—	—	—	—
	2014	185	—	35	—	—	—	—	—	—	—	—	—	—	—	—	—	—	—
Qatar	2013	—	—	—	—	—	—	—	—	—	—	—	—	—	—	1 600	—	—	—
Syrian Arab Republic	2012	—	—	—	—	—	—	—	—	—	498	—	—	—	—	—	—	—	—

Country or territory, by region / Year	Acetic anhydride (litres)	N-Acetylanthranilic acid (kilograms)	Ephedrine (kilograms)	Ephedrine preparations[a] (kilograms)	Ergometrine (grams)	Ergotamine (grams)	Isosafrole (litres)	Lysergic acid (grams)	3,4-Methylenedioxyphenyl-2-propanone (litres)	1-Phenyl-2-propanone (litres)	Norephedrine (phenylpropanolamine) (kilograms)	Phenylacetic acid (kilograms)	alpha-phenylacetoacetonitrile[b] (kilograms)	Piperonal (kilograms)	Potassium permanganate (kilograms)	Pseudoephedrine (kilograms)	Pseudoephedrine preparations[a] (kilograms)	Safrole (litres)
Turkey[f]																		
2010	11 104[f]	—	—	—	—	—	—	—	—	—	—	—	—	—	—	—	—	—
2011	3 706	—	—	—	—	—	—	—	—	—	—	—	—	—	—	—	—	—
2012	177	—	—	°	—	—	—	—	—	—	—	—	—	—	—	—	—	—
2013	14 672	—	—	—	—	—	—	—	—	—	—	—	—	—	—	—	—	—
2014	854	—	33	—	—	—	—	—	—	—	—	—	—	—	—	—	—	—
Uzbekistan																		
2010	—	—	—	—	—	—	—	—	—	—	—	—	—	—	626	—	—	—
2011	—	—	—	—	—	—	—	—	—	—	—	—	—	—	3	—	—	—
2013	—	—	—	—	—	—	—	—	—	—	—	—	—	—	160	—	—	—
2014	—	—	—	—	—	—	—	—	—	—	—	—	—	—	52	—	—	—
Regional total																		
2010	**50 560**	**0**	**3 003**	**°**	**0**	**0**	**0**	**0**	**0**	**0**	**0**	**0**	**0**	**0**	**3 911**	**0**	**0**	**0**
2011	**71 994**	**0**	**4 104**	**0**	**0**	**0**	**0**	**0**	**0**	**0**	**0**	**0**	**0**	**0**	**1 253**	**0**	**0**	**0**
2012	**32 501**	**0**	**6**	**20**	**0**	**0**	**0**	**0**	**0**	**498**	**0**	**0**	**0**	**0**	**0**	**0**	**0**	**0**
2013	**60 866**	**0**	**54**	**0**	**0**	**0**	**0**	**0**	**0**	**0**	**0**	**0**	**0**	**0**	**1 760**	**0**	**0**	**0**
2014	**8 790**	**0**	**68**	**0**	**0**	**0**	**0**	**0**	**0**	**0**	**0**	**0**	**0**	**0**	**52**	**0**	**0**	**0**

Europe

States not members of the European Union

Country or territory / Year	Acetic anhydride (litres)	N-Acetylanthranilic acid (kilograms)	Ephedrine (kilograms)	Ephedrine preparations[a] (kilograms)	Ergometrine (grams)	Ergotamine (grams)	Isosafrole (litres)	Lysergic acid (grams)	3,4-Methylenedioxyphenyl-2-propanone (litres)	1-Phenyl-2-propanone (litres)	Norephedrine (phenylpropanolamine) (kilograms)	Phenylacetic acid (kilograms)	alpha-phenylacetoacetonitrile[b] (kilograms)	Piperonal (kilograms)	Potassium permanganate (kilograms)	Pseudoephedrine (kilograms)	Pseudoephedrine preparations[a] (kilograms)	Safrole (litres)
Belarus																		
2010	—	—	—	°	—	—	—	—	2	—	—	—	—	—	—	16	°	—
2011	°	—	—	°	—	—	—	—	—	—	1	—	—	—	—	—	—	—
2012	—	—	—	—	—	—	—	—	—	—	—	—	—	—	—	—	°	—
2013	—	—	—	—	—	—	—	—	—	—	—	—	—	—	—	1	—	—
2014	—	—	—	—	—	—	—	—	—	—	—	—	—	—	—	—	—	—
Norway																		
2010	—	—	—	1	—	—	—	—	—	—	—	—	—	—	—	—	—	—
2012	—	—	—	1	—	—	—	—	—	—	—	—	—	—	—	—	—	—
Republic of Moldova																		
2013	—	—	—	°	—	—	—	—	—	—	—	—	—	—	—	—	—	—
2014	—	—	—	—	—	—	—	—	—	—	—	—	—	—	—	—	[a]	—

Country or territory, by region / Year	Acetic anhydride (litres)	N-Acetylanthranilic acid (kilograms)	Ephedrine (kilograms)	Ephedrine preparations[a] (kilograms)	Ergometrine (grams)	Ergotamine (grams)	Isosafrole (litres)	Lysergic acid (grams)	3,4-Methylenedioxyphenyl-2-propanone (litres)	1-Phenyl-2-propanone (litres)	Norephedrine (phenylpropanolamine) (kilograms)	Phenylacetic acid (kilograms)	alpha-phenylacetoacetonitrile[b] (kilograms)	Piperonal (kilograms)	Potassium permanganate (kilograms)	Pseudoephedrine (kilograms)	Pseudoephedrine preparations[a] (kilograms)	Safrole (litres)
Russian Federation																		
2010	15	—	—	—	—	—	—	—	—	—	—	—	—	—	°	—	—	—
2011	820	—	°	—	—	—	—	102	—	1 060	—	—	—	—	—	3	—	—
2012	5	—	°	—	—	—	—	—	—	4	—	—	—	—	—	—	—	—
2013	8	—	2	°	—	—	—	83	—	30	—	—	—	—	—	—	—	—
2014	17	—	—	—	—	—	—	—	—	°	—	—	—	—	—	—	°	—
Serbia																		
2012	—	—	°	—	—	—	—	—	—	—	—	—	—	°	—	—	—	—
Switzerland																		
2014	—	—	—	a	—	—	—	—	—	—	—	—	—	—	—	—	—	—
Ukraine																		
2010	43	—	8	°	—	—	—	—	—	°	—	—	—	—	386	17	3	—
2011	31	—	4	5	—	—	—	—	—	5	°	—	—	—	396	2	2	—
2012	52	—	—	°	—	—	—	—	—	°	°	—	—	—	101	°	—	—
2013	1 664	—	—	51	—	—	—	—	—	—	°	—	—	—	225	—	2 991	—
States members of the European Union																		
Austria																		
2010	—	—	—	—	—	—	—	—	—	—	—	—	—	—	—	1	—	—
2013	2	—	—	—	—	—	—	—	104	—	—	—	—	—	1	—	—	—
2014	—	—	—	—	—	—	—	—	—	—	—	—	—	—	1	—	—	—
Belgium																		
2010	—	—	—	—	—	—	—	—	—	5 050	—	—	—	—	—	—	—	—
2011	—	—	—	—	—	—	—	—	—	—	—	—	—	—	—	—	—	1
2012	—	—	1	—	—	—	—	—	2 781	503	—	—	—	—	—	—	—	—
2013	—	—	2	—	—	—	—	—	5	15	—	—	—	—	—	—	—	—
2014	—	—	—	—	—	—	—	—	—	25	—	—	122	—	—	—	—	—
Bulgaria																		
2010	21 111	—	—	—	—	—	—	—	—	20	—	—	—	—	—	—	—	—
2011	20	—	—	—	—	—	—	—	—	545	—	—	—	—	—	—	—	—
2012	42	—	°	—	—	—	—	—	—	2	—	—	—	—	—	—	—	—

Country or territory, by region / Year	Acetic anhydride (litres)	N-Acetylanthranilic acid (kilograms)	Ephedrine (kilograms)	Ephedrine preparations[a] (kilograms)	Ergometrine (grams)	Ergotamine (grams)	Isosafrole (litres)	Lysergic acid (grams)	3,4-Methylenedioxyphenyl-2-propanone (litres)	1-Phenyl-2-propanone (litres)	Norephedrine (phenylpropanolamine) (kilograms)	Phenylacetic acid (kilograms)	alpha-phenylacetoacetonitrile[b] (kilograms)	Piperonal (kilograms)	Potassium permanganate (kilograms)	Pseudoephedrine (kilograms)	Pseudoephedrine preparations[a] (kilograms)	Safrole (litres)
2013	–	–	–	–	–	–	–	–	–	–	–	97	–	–	–	–	108	–
2014	–	–	–	–	–	–	–	–	–	–	–	–	1 980	–	–	–	841	–
Croatia																		
2011	–	–	°	°	–	–	–	–	–	–	–	–	–	–	–	–	–	–
2013	–	–	–	°	–	–	–	–	–	°	–	–	–	–	–	–	–	–
2014	–	–	–	°	–	–	–	–	–	–	–	–	–	–	–	–	°	–
Czech Republic																		
2010	–	–	7	–	–	–	–	–	–	–	–	–	–	–	–	2	–	–
2011	–	–	4	–	–	–	–	–	–	–	–	–	–	–	–	6	–	–
2012	–	–	3	–	–	–	–	–	–	–	–	–	–	–	–	2	16	–
2013	–	–	°	–	–	–	–	–	–	–	–	–	–	–	–	64	25	–
2014	–	–	14	2	–	–	–	–	–	–	–	–	–	–	–	12	351	–
Estonia																		
2010	–	–	–	°	–	–	–	–	–	29	–	–	–	–	–	–	–	–
2011	–	–	–	–	–	–	–	–	–	10	–	–	–	–	–	–	–	–
2013	–	–	–	°	–	–	–	–	–	°	–	100	–	–	–	–	–	–
2014	°	–	–	–	–	–	–	–	–	–	–	–	5	–	–	–	–	–
Finland																		
2011	–	–	–	–	–	–	–	–	–	3	–	–	–	–	–	–	–	–
2012	–	–	–	–	–	–	–	–	–	°	–	–	–	–	–	–	–	–
2013	–	–	–	600	–	–	–	–	–	°	–	–	–	–	–	–	–	–
2014	–	–	–	°	–	–	–	–	–	°	–	–	–	–	–	–	–	–
France																		
2010	–	–	°	–	–	–	–	–	–	°	–	–	–	–	1	°	–	–
2011	–	–	1	–	–	–	–	–	–	°	–	–	–	–	–	–	–	–
2012	–	–	1	–	–	–	–	–	–	°	–	–	–	–	1	1	–	–
2013	–	–	°	–	–	–	–	–	–	°	–	–	–	–	–	°	–	–
2014	–	–	15	–	–	–	–	–	–	1	–	–	–	–	–	–	–	–
Germany																		
2010	12	–	46	–	–	–	°	–	–	–	°	2	–	–	°	°	–	–
2011	3	–	20	–	–	–	–	–	–	24	°	6 000	–	–	–	3	–	–

73

Country or territory, by region	Year	Acetic anhydride (litres)	N-Acetylanthranilic acid (kilograms)	Ephedrine (kilograms)	Ephedrine preparations[a] (kilograms)	Ergometrine (grams)	Ergotamine (grams)	Isosafrole (litres)	Lysergic acid (grams)	3,4-Methylenedioxyphenyl-2-propanone (litres)	1-Phenyl-2-propanone (litres)	Norephedrine (phenylpropanolamine) (kilograms)	Phenylacetic acid (kilograms)	alpha-phenylacetoacetonitrile[b] (kilograms)	Piperonal (kilograms)	Potassium permanganate (kilograms)	Pseudoephedrine (kilograms)	Pseudoephedrine preparations[a] (kilograms)	Safrole (litres)
	2012	–	–	°	–	–	–	–	–	–	38	–	–	–	–	°	–	–	–
	2013	–	–	1	–	–	–	–	–	–	°	–	–	5 105	–	1	–	°	–
	2014	–	–	°	–	–	–	–	–	–	2	–	–	–	–	1	–	–	–
Greece	2012	–	–	°	–	–	–	–	–	–	–	–	–	–	–	–	–	–	–
	2013	–	–	°	–	–	–	–	–	–	–	–	–	–	–	–	–	–	–
Hungary	2010	–	–	°	1	–	–	–	–	–	–	–	–	–	–	–	–	7	–
	2011	33	–	–	1	–	–	–	–	–	–	–	–	–	–	–	–	–	–
	2012	–	–	–	°	–	–	–	–	–	–	–	–	–	–	–	–	–	–
	2013	–	–	°	–	–	–	–	–	–	–	–	–	–	4	–	–	–	–
	2014	–	–	–	1	–	–	–	–	–	–	–	–	–	–	–	–	–	–
Ireland	2011	–	–	–	3	–	–	–	449	–	–	–	–	–	–	–	–	–	–
	2012	–	–	–	–	–	–	–	–	3	–	–	–	–	–	–	–	–	–
	2014	–	–	–	–	–	–	–	–	–	22	–	–	–	–	–	–	–	–
Latvia	2011	–	–	–	–	–	–	–	–	–	–	–	–	–	–	–	–	–	–
Lithuania	2011	–	–	–	–	–	–	–	–	1	600	–	–	–	332	–	–	–	–
	2012	–	–	–	–	–	–	–	–	–	17	–	–	–	–	–	–	–	–
	2013	–	–	–	–	–	–	–	–	–	15	–	–	–	–	–	–	–	13
	2014	–	–	–	–	–	–	–	–	–	690	–	–	–	–	–	–	–	–
Luxembourg	2010	–	–	–	–	–	–	–	–	–	–	–	–	–	–	–	–	77	–
	2012	–	–	–	–	–	–	–	–	–	–	–	–	–	–	–	300	–	–
Netherlands	2010	–	–	500	–	–	–	–	–	–	334	–	–	–	–	–	–	8	85
	2011	–	–	–	–	–	–	–	–	–	111	–	–	–	–	–	–	–	105
	2012	–	–	–	–	–	–	10	–	–	123	–	–	–	–	–	500	–	–

Country or territory, by region	Year	Acetic anhydride (litres)	N-Acetylanthranilic acid (kilograms)	Ephedrine (kilograms)	Ephedrine preparations[a] (kilograms)	Ergometrine (grams)	Ergotamine (grams)	Isosafrole (litres)	Lysergic acid (grams)	3,4-Methylenedioxyphenyl-2-propanone (litres)	1-Phenyl-2-propanone (litres)	Norephedrine (phenylpropanolamine) (kilograms)	Phenylacetic acid (kilograms)	alpha-phenylacetoacetonitrile[b] (kilograms)	Piperonal (kilograms)	Potassium permanganate (kilograms)	Pseudoephedrine (kilograms)	Pseudoephedrine preparations[a] (kilograms)	Safrole (litres)
	2013	—	—	—	—	—	—	10	—	112	428	—	—	3 090	5	80	—	—	13 825
	2014	—	—	—	—	—	—	—	—	—	—	—	—	—	—	—	—	2	—
Poland	2010	—	—	—	—	—	—	—	—	—	60	—	—	—	—	—	—	—	—
	2011	1	—	—	—	—	—	—	—	—	350	—	—	—	—	—	290	—	—
	2012	1 755	1	10	—	—	—	—	—	—	149	—	116	—	—	5	—	—	—
	2013	°	—	°	—	—	—	—	—	—	1	—	—	611	—	—	1	—	—
	2014	4	—	—	—	—	—	—	—	—	1 472	—	—	—	—	—	—	—	—
Portugal	2013	—	—	1	—	—	—	—	—	—	—	—	—	—	—	—	°	—	—
Romania	2013	—	—	—	—	—	—	—	—	—	—	—	—	150	1	—	—	—	—
	2014	—	—	—	—	—	—	—	—	—	—	—	—	—	—	—	—	—	—
Slovakia	2010	—	—	°	—	—	—	—	—	—	—	—	—	—	—	—	°	—	—
	2011	6 020	—	°	—	—	—	—	—	—	—	—	—	—	—	—	°	—	—
	2012	—	—	°	—	—	—	—	—	—	—	—	—	—	—	—	°	—	—
	2013	—	—	—	—	—	—	—	—	—	—	—	—	—	—	°	°	11	—
	2014	—	—	°	—	—	—	—	—	—	—	—	—	—	—	—	—	—	—
Slovenia	2012	—	—	°	—	—	—	—	°	—	—	—	—	—	—	—	—	—	—
	2013	—	—	°	—	—	—	—	912	—	—	—	—	—	—	°	—	—	—
Spain	2010	—	—	°	—	—	—	—	—	—	—	—	—	—	—	2	—	—	—
	2011	11	—	1 500	—	—	—	—	—	—	—	—	—	—	—	1	—	—	—
	2012	9 497	—	—	°	—	—	—	—	—	—	—	—	—	—	19	—	—	—
	2013	110	—	—	—	—	1	—	—	—	—	—	—	—	1 400	5 926	—	—	—
	2014	—	—	—	—	—	—	—	—	—	—	—	—	—	—	—	—	—	—

Country or territory, by region	Year	Acetic anhydride (litres)	N-Acetylanthranilic acid (kilograms)	Ephedrine (kilograms)	Ephedrine preparations[a] (kilograms)	Ergometrine (grams)	Ergotamine (grams)	Isosafrole (litres)	Lysergic acid (grams)	3,4-Methylenedioxyphenyl-2-propanone (litres)	1-Phenyl-2-propanone (litres)	Norephedrine (phenylpropanolamine) (kilograms)	Phenylacetic acid (kilograms)	alpha-phenylacetoacetonitrile[b] (kilograms)	Piperonal (kilograms)	Potassium permanganate (kilograms)	Pseudoephedrine (kilograms)	Pseudoephedrine preparations[a] (kilograms)	Safrole (litres)
Sweden	2010	—	—	—	—	—	—	—	—	—	—	—	—	—	—	1	—	—	—
	2011	—	—	—	2	—	—	—	—	—	—	—	—	—	—	—	—	—	—
	2012	—	—	—	1	—	—	—	—	—	—	—	—	—	°	—	—	—	—
	2013	—	—	—	1	—	—	—	—	—	—	—	—	—	—	—	—	—	—
	2014	—	—	—	3	—	—	—	—	—	—	—	—	—	—	—	—	—	—
United Kingdom	2010	—	—	1	—	—	—	—	—	—	—	—	—	—	10	—	—	—	—
	2011	—	—	500	—	—	—	—	—	—	—	—	—	—	—	—	—	—	—
	2012	1	1	—	—	—	—	—	—	—	—	—	—	—	—	—	—	a	—
	2013	—	—	—	—	—	—	—	—	—	—	—	—	—	—	—	—	—	—
Regional total	**2010**	**21 181**	**0**	**563**	**2**	**0**	**0**	**°**	**102**	**2**	**5 493**	**1**	**2**	**0**	**0**	**390**	**36**	**94**	**85**
	2011	**6 894**	**0**	**530**	**11**	**0**	**0**	**0**	**449**	**1**	**2 708**	**1**	**6 000**	**0**	**10**	**396**	**304**	**2**	**106**
	2012	**1 899**	**1**	**1 504**	**2**	**0**	**°**	**10**	**0**	**3**	**836**	**°**	**116**	**0**	**332**	**121**	**804**	**16**	**0**
	2013	**11 171**	**1**	**15**	**653**	**0**	**1**	**10**	**83**	**3 910**	**61**	**°**	**97**	**0**	**1 405**	**6 239**	**64**	**3 125**	**13 838**
	2014	**131**	**0**	**31**	**7**	**0**	**0**	**0**	**0**	**5**	**2 640**	**0**	**100**	**11 062**	**5**	**1**	**13**	**1 206**	**0**
Oceania																			
Australia	2010	—	—	46	51	—	100	1	4	°	9	11	—	—	°	—	303	366	47
	2011	6	—	261	5	—	4	°	—	1	—	1	10	—	°	—	724	723	2 565
	2012	2	—	520	—	—	—	°	691	°	1	2	°	—	°	—	770	2	1
	2013	—	—	1 253	—	—	207	°	523	20	1	1	°	—	°	—	629	—	11
	2014	—	—	457	—	—	57	°	—	—	—	°	°	—	°	—	11	—	184
Fiji	2010	—	—	—	—	—	—	—	—	—	—	—	—	—	—	—	—	18	—
New Zealand	2010	°	—	—	24	—	—	—	—	—	—	—	—	—	—	1	—	925	35
	2011	°	—	—	96	—	—	—	—	—	—	—	—	—	—	°	—	608	—
	2012	°	—	—	5	—	—	—	—	—	—	—	—	—	—	°	—	426	1
	2013	°	—	—	3	—	—	—	—	—	—	—	—	—	—	—	—	691	—

Country or territory, by region	Year	Acetic anhydride (litres)	N-Acetylanthranilic acid (kilograms)	Ephedrine (kilograms)	Ephedrine preparations[a] (kilograms)	Ergometrine (grams)	Ergotamine (grams)	Isosafrole (litres)	Lysergic acid (grams)	3,4-Methylenedioxyphenyl-2-propanone (litres)	1-Phenyl-2-propanone (litres)	Norephedrine (phenylpropanolamine) (kilograms)	Phenylacetic acid (kilograms)	alpha-phenylacetoacetonitrile[b] (kilograms)	Piperonal (kilograms)	Potassium permanganate (kilograms)	Pseudoephedrine (kilograms)	Pseudoephedrine preparations[a] (kilograms)	Safrole (litres)
Regional total																			
	2010	0	0	46	75	0	100	1	4	0	9	11	0	0	0	1	303	1 309	83
	2011	6	0	261	101	0	4	0	0	1	0	1	10	0	0	0	724	1 332	2 565
	2012	2	0	520	5	0	0	0	691	0	0	2	0	0	0	0	770	429	2
	2013	0	0	1 253	3	0	207	0	523	0	1	1	0	0	0	0	629	691	11
	2014	0	0	457	0	0	57	0	0	20	1	0	0	0	0	0	11	0	184
World total																			
	2010	155 656	13	22 262	110	2 000	79 080	1	106	2	26 403	62	234 329	0	0	32 107	17 900	2 170	169
	2011	197 744	0	33 326	33 797	0	824	0	521	124	5 312	2	1 022 231	0	10	38 406	6 398	2 291	17 122
	2012	89 657	1	7 624	2 714	0	1 650	10	694	228	6 818	286	1 700	0	336	92 702	30 481	1 583	2 028
	2013	175 739	1	13 256	6 721	0	657	10	606	3 927	8 292	23	10 068	0	1 405	57 566	15 571	7 534	14 115
	2014	44 971	0	32 772	3 261	0	57	2 100	57	58	16 575	58	51 066	11 062	5	173 823	351	1 326	184

[a] Seizures of ephedrine and pseudoephedrine reported to the Board in consumption units (such as tablets and doses) have not been converted into kilograms, as the actual quantity of ephedrine and pseudoephedrine is not known. The following countries have reported seizures of preparations containing ephedrine and/or pseudoephedrine quantified in terms of consumption units:

	Year	Ephedrine preparations (units)	Pseudoephedrine preparations (units)
Bulgaria	2010	4 252	–
China, Hong Kong SAR	2012	50 000	3 660
Côte d'Ivoire	2013	–	656 271
	2011	23 962	–
	2012	80 820	–
Czech Republic	2010	15 000	326 941
	2011	2 570	872 703
Finland	2010	10 075	–
	2011	6 107	–
	2012	6 359	–
Germany	2010	170	462
	2011	–	1 890
	2013	4 034	78
Greece	2010	2	–
	2011	8	–
Guatemala	2010	–	1 470 015

	Year	Ephedrine preparations (units)	Pseudoephedrine preparations (units)
Indonesia	2011	3 000	–
	2012	53	–
	2014	17	–
Ireland	2010	2 200	–
Lebanon	2014	47	7 662
New Zealand	2011	123 431	34 833
	2012	–	3 630
	2013	6 956	5 073
Republic of Moldova	2014	–	60
Slovakia	2010	–	336
	2011	–	1 734
	2013	–	16 128
Sweden	2012	60 976	–
Switzerland	2014	185	–
Thailand	2010	–	33 376 072
	2011	–	10 240 820
	2012	–	2 011 100
	2013	–	302 630
United Kingdom	2010	432 300	1 000
	2011	288 000	–
	2013	–	1 000
United States	2010	2 574	2 309 242
	2011	–	4 003 371

[b] Included in Table I of the 1988 Convention, effective 9 October 2014.

[c] Figures reported for the United States for 2011 may inadvertently include sizeable seizures of *Sida cordifolia* and/or *Ephedra* plant extracts and are thus not comparable with figures for previous years.

[d] For statistical purposes, the data for China do not include those for China, Hong Kong Special Administrative Region (SAR), and China, Macao SAR.

[e] Based on data on seizures of precursors reported annually since 2010 by the Drug Control Headquarters of the Islamic Republic of Iran in the *Drug Control Report*.

[f] Turkish National Police, Anti-Smuggling and Organized Crime Department, *Turkish Report of Anti-Smuggling and Organized Crime: 2011* (Ankara, 2012).

Table A.2. Seizures of substances in Table II of the 1988 Convention as reported to the International Narcotics Control Board, 2010-2014

Country or territory, by region	Year	Acetone (litres)	Anthranilic acid (kilograms)	Ethyl ether (litres)	Hydrochloric acid (litres)	Methyl ethyl ketone (litres)	Piperidine (litres)	Sulphuric acid (litres)	Toluene (litres)
Africa									
Nigeria	2011	400	—	—	—	—	—	25	200
Regional total	2010	0	0	0	0	0	0	0	0
	2011	400	0	0	0	0	0	25	200
	2012	0	0	0	0	0	0	0	0
	2013	0	0	0	0	0	0	0	0
	2014	0	0	0	0	0	0	0	0
Americas									
Central America and the Caribbean									
Guatemala	2011	—	—	—	8 707	—	—	212	—
Honduras	2011	—	—	—	a	—	—	—	—
Regional total	2010	0	0	0	0	0	0	0	0
	2011	0	0	0	8 707	0	0	212	0
	2012	0	0	0	0	0	0	0	0
	2013	0	0	0	0	0	0	0	0
	2014	0	0	0	0	0	0	0	0
North America									
Canada	2010	172	—	—	267	4	—	55	423
	2011	371	—	49	274	4	°	201	1 825
	2012	2 786	—	°	855	4	18	24	1 718
	2013	569	—	—	48	—	—	2	981

Country or territory, by region	Year	Acetone (litres)	Anthranilic acid (kilograms)	Ethyl ether (litres)	Hydrochloric acid (litres)	Methyl ethyl ketone (litres)	Piperidine (litres)	Sulphuric acid (litres)	Toluene (litres)
Mexico	2010	7 776	–	47	10 244	370	–	2 927	21 451
	2011	23 262	–	219	78 125	–	–	1 652	49 410
	2012	10 669	–	14	29 310	64	–	3 171	26 243
	2013	6 901	–	28 001	14 207	94	–	439	12 333
	2014	2 402	–	0	8 446	281	–	1 406	4 324
United States of America	2010	55 390	–	25 258	69 940	15	90	28 387	1 305
	2011	71 142	–	115	109 602	29	11	1 231 111	262
	2012	10 594	–	60	206	3	189	125	12
	2013	2 457	–	18	1 681	11	57	1 930	102
	2014	4 477	–	277	1 326	11	57	1	72
Regional total	**2010**	**63 338**	**0**	**25 306**	**80 451**	**389**	**90**	**31 369**	**23 179**
	2011	**94 775**	**0**	**384**	**188 001**	**32**	**12**	**1 232 965**	**51 497**
	2012	**24 049**	**0**	**74**	**30 372**	**71**	**207**	**3 320**	**27 972**
	2013	**9 926**	**0**	**28 019**	**15 936**	**104**	**57**	**2 371**	**13 415**
	2014	**6 879**	**0**	**278**	**9 772**	**292**	**57**	**1 407**	**4 396**
South America									
Argentina	2010	214	–	237	163	–	–	17	1
	2011	245	–	182	96	2	–	16	–
	2012	311	–	131	52	53	–	26	–
	2013	2 768	–	104	165	3	–	202	–
	2014	67	–	77	24 677	–	–	50	–
Bolivia (Plurinational State of)	2011	51 663	–	87	9 307	176	–	201 621	5 590
	2012	59 711	–	7 120	5 873	680	–	72 034	6 349
	2013	99 315	–	–	24 839	57	–	67 929	140
	2014	18 830	–	1 112	5 700	–	–	56 283	126
Brazil	2010	956	–	–	22 381	6 714	–	1 834	6 748
	2011	954	–	128	7 211	96	–	4 747	49

Country or territory, by region	Year	Acetone (litres)	Anthranilic acid (kilograms)	Ethyl ether (litres)	Hydrochloric acid (litres)	Methyl ethyl ketone (litres)	Piperidine (litres)	Sulphuric acid (litres)	Toluene (litres)
	2012	1 606	–	466	91 697	3 308	–	28 271	3 742
	2013	2 491	–	58	5 948	–	–	698	–
	2014	154	–	–	15 319		–	399	
Chile	2010	1 600	–	–	–	–	–	2 223	–
	2011	–	–	–	19	–	–	93	–
	2012	–	–	–	–	–	–	5	–
	2013	2	–	–	144	–	–	63 610	–
	2014	25	–	4	226	–	–	233	–
Colombia	2010	688 224	–	6 455	187 914	44 160	–	631 247	66 060
	2011	463 883	–	1 541	96 660	–	–	201 812	42 044
	2012	739 247	–	25 295	76 290	1 419	–	163 242	33 792
	2013	482 063	–	2 286	144 686	3 406	–	1 060 578	765
	2014	456 643	–	2 117	75 058	6 155	–	276 004	191 390
Ecuador	2010	4 320	–	–	2 286	10 774	–	1 473	–
	2011	–	–	–	931	2 400	–	3 954	–
	2012	–	–	–	–	–	–	771	–
	2013	–	–	–	104	1 420	–	1 625	–
	2014	–	–	–	154	–	–	708	–
Paraguay	2011	4 500	–	5	833	–	–	5 229	2 650
	2013	–	–	–	2 019	–	–	6 960	–
Peru	2010	31 139	–	–	172 807	–	–	31 367	–
	2011	32 456	–	45	145 850	310	–	28 505	1 919
	2012	70 024	–	–	87 695	–	–	29 777	100
	2013	86 313	–	128	73 200	157	–	87 675	–
	2014	83 006	–	4	58 907	1 225	–	87 305	3 128
Venezuela (Bolivarian Republic of)	2011	15 858	–	–	25 781	1 140	–	30 284	1 200
	2012	39 331	–	–	28 605	–	–	87 470	427
	2014	27 598	–	–	1 061	99	–	831	–

Country or territory, by region	Year	Acetone (litres)	Anthranilic acid (kilograms)	Ethyl ether (litres)	Hydrochloric acid (litres)	Methyl ethyl ketone (litres)	Piperidine (litres)	Sulphuric acid (litres)	Toluene (litres)
Regional total	2010	726 452	0	6 693	385 550	61 648	0	668 162	72 809
	2011	569 558	0	1 987	286 687	4 123	0	476 261	53 452
	2012	910 230	0	33 012	290 212	5 460	0	381 596	44 411
	2013	672 952	0	2 577	251 104	5 043	0	1 289 277	905
	2014	586 323	0	3 313	181 101	7 479	0	421 813	194 644

Asia

East and South-East Asia

Country or territory, by region	Year	Acetone (litres)	Anthranilic acid (kilograms)	Ethyl ether (litres)	Hydrochloric acid (litres)	Methyl ethyl ketone (litres)	Piperidine (litres)	Sulphuric acid (litres)	Toluene (litres)
China[b]	2010	31 966	–	16 572	141 918	1 403	–	219 388	–
	2011	21 474	–	17 980	150 165	1 391	–	23 024	–
	2012	31 953	–	15 770	166 825	1 217	–	18 479	13 900
	2013	351 870	490 302	12 204	1 627 816	1 906	2	1 297 043	221 026
	2014	139 171	816	7 918	1 659 718	640	–	679 966	290 917
China, Hong Kong SAR	2010	–	–		570	–	–	–	–
Indonesia	2011	2	–	–	10	–	–	1	3
	2012	2	–	–	6	–	–	5	–
	2013	1	–	–		–	–	–	–
	2014	1	–	–	2 376	–	–	1 015	506
Malaysia	2010	130	–	–	120	–	–	5	725
	2011	800	–	45	800	–	–	–	950
	2012	460	–	–	300	–	–	100	150
	2013	85	–	9	219	–	–	–	25
	2014	139	–	13	779	–	–	–	153
Myanmar	2010	1 202	–	600	–	–	–	2 000	–
	2013	–	–	–	145	–	–	924	–
	2014	193 922	–	–	1 687 325	–	–	6 716 899	2 452 409

Country or territory, by region	Year	Acetone (litres)	Anthranilic acid (kilograms)	Ethyl ether (litres)	Hydrochloric acid (litres)	Methyl ethyl ketone (litres)	Piperidine (litres)	Sulphuric acid (litres)	Toluene (litres)
Philippines	2010	55	–	–	105	–	–	–	300
	2011	21	–	°	11	–	–	1	31 313
	2012	6 436	–	5	1 646	25	–	3 080	17 941
	2013	–	–	–	–	–	–	10	–
	2014	°	–	–	°	–	–	–	640
Singapore	2014	20	–	–	–	–	–	–	–
Thailand	2011	1	–	–	°	–	–	163	1
	2012	300	–	–	–	–	–	–	450
	2013	–	–	–	450	–	–	–	–
Regional total	**2010**	**33 353**	**0**	**16 572**	**142 713**	**1 403**	**0**	**221 394**	**1 025**
	2011	**22 298**	**0**	**18 025**	**150 986**	**1 391**	**0**	**23 188**	**32 267**
	2012	**39 151**	**0**	**15 775**	**168 776**	**1 242**	**2**	**21 664**	**32 441**
	2013	**351 956**	**490 302**	**12 813**	**1 628 630**	**1 906**	**0**	**1 297 977**	**221 051**
	2014	**333 253**	**816**	**7 931**	**3 350 198**	**640**	**0**	**7 397 880**	**2 744 624**

South Asia

Country or territory, by region	Year	Acetone (litres)	Anthranilic acid (kilograms)	Ethyl ether (litres)	Hydrochloric acid (litres)	Methyl ethyl ketone (litres)	Piperidine (litres)	Sulphuric acid (litres)	Toluene (litres)
Bangladesh	2010	120	–	–	–	22 767	–	–	6
Maldives	2010	–	–	–	–	–	–	7 331[c]	–
	2011	–	–	–	14	–	–	5	–
Regional total	**2010**	**120**	**0**	**0**	**0**	**22 767**	**0**	**7 331**	**6**
	2011	**0**	**0**	**0**	**14**	**0**	**0**	**5**	**0**
	2012	**0**	**0**	**0**	**0**	**0**	**0**	**0**	**0**
	2013	**0**	**0**	**0**	**0**	**0**	**0**	**0**	**0**
	2014	**0**	**0**	**0**	**0**	**0**	**0**	**0**	**0**

Country or territory, by region / Year	Acetone (litres)	Anthranilic acid (kilograms)	Ethyl ether (litres)	Hydrochloric acid (litres)	Methyl ethyl ketone (litres)	Piperidine (litres)	Sulphuric acid (litres)	Toluene (litres)
West Asia								
Afghanistan								
2010	–	–	–	5 286	–	–	–	–
2011	–	–	–	120	–	–	–	–
2012	–	–	–	–	–	–	3 764	–
2013	174	–	–	4 705	–	–	–	–
2014	–	–	–	5 317	–	–	19 075	25
Armenia								
2011	°	–	–	°	–	–	°	–
2012	–	–	–	°	–	–	–	–
2013	–	–	°	°	–	–	–	–
2014	–	–	°	°	–	–	–	–
Kazakhstan								
2010	245	–	–	51 794	–	–	–	–
2011	78	–	–	10 707	–	–	698	–
2012	1	–	–	1 600	–	–	913	–
Kyrgyzstan								
2010	–	–	–	–	–	–	94	–
2012	–	–	–	98	–	–	3 703	–
2013	–	–	–	–	–	–	4 386	–
2014	–	–	–	535	–	–	12 756	–
Lebanon								
2010	–	–	°	°	–	–	–	–
2011	–	–	°	–	–	–	–	–
2012	13	–	2 358	–	–	–	–	–
2014	32	–	43	10	–	–	–	–
Pakistan								
2010	–	–	–	7 110	–	–	326	–
2012	–	–	–	–	–	–	–	–
2013	–	–	–	925	–	–	326	–
2014	–	–	–	9 996	–	–	27 367	–

Country or territory, by region	Year	Acetone (litres)	Anthranilic acid (kilograms)	Ethyl ether (litres)	Hydrochloric acid (litres)	Methyl ethyl ketone (litres)	Piperidine (litres)	Sulphuric acid (litres)	Toluene (litres)
Qatar	2013	565	—	—	407 363	—	°	443 814	597
Tajikistan	2011	—	—	—	—	—	—	6 803	—
	2012	—	—	—	—	14	—	1	—
Turkey	2011	3	—	—	—	—	—	°	—
Uzbekistan	2011	274	—	—	40	—	—	2 540	—
	2014	—	—	—	—	—	—	1 610	—
Regional total	**2010**	**245**	**0**	**0**	**64 190**	**0**	**0**	**94**	**0**
	2011	**354**	**0**	**0**	**10 867**	**0**	**0**	**10 040**	**0**
	2012	**14**	**0**	**2 358**	**1 698**	**14**	**0**	**8 707**	**0**
	2013	**739**	**0**	**0**	**412 993**	**0**	**0**	**448 526**	**597**
	2014	**32**	**0**	**43**	**15 859**	**0**	**0**	**60 809**	**25**

Europe

States not members of the European Union

Country or territory, by region	Year	Acetone (litres)	Anthranilic acid (kilograms)	Ethyl ether (litres)	Hydrochloric acid (litres)	Methyl ethyl ketone (litres)	Piperidine (litres)	Sulphuric acid (litres)	Toluene (litres)
Belarus	2010	—	—	—	2	2	—	—	—
	2013	—	—	—	—	—	—	10 751	—
	2014	94	—	—	—	—	—	—	—
Bosnia and Herzegovina	2010	—	—	—	—	—	—	550	—
Russian Federation	2010	555	—	7	846	—	—	54	118
	2011	—	—	—	48	—	—	66	—
	2012	—	—	—	26	—	—	91 433	—
	2013	—	—	—	5	—	—	15	—
	2014	—	—	—	1	—	—	7	—

Country or territory, by region	Year	Acetone (litres)	Anthranilic acid (kilograms)	Ethyl ether (litres)	Hydrochloric acid (litres)	Methyl ethyl ketone (litres)	Piperidine (litres)	Sulphuric acid (litres)	Toluene (litres)
Ukraine	2010	20 726	—	°	111 221	131	—	112 410	26 235
	2011	1 821	—	555	24 608	1 706	—	281 755	4 245
	2012	10 324	—	9 216	2 211	720	—	3 302	20 089
	2013	1 163	—	—	3 053	—	—	631	602

States members of the European Union

Country or territory, by region	Year	Acetone (litres)	Anthranilic acid (kilograms)	Ethyl ether (litres)	Hydrochloric acid (litres)	Methyl ethyl ketone (litres)	Piperidine (litres)	Sulphuric acid (litres)	Toluene (litres)
Austria	2010	—	—	—	1	—	—	—	16
	2011	°	—	1	°	—	—	2	—
	2012	—	—	°	—	18	—	—	1
	2013	3	—	—	9	—	—	—	6
	2014	1	—	—	18	—	—	121	73
Belgium	2010	—	—	—	1 016	—	—	100	—
	2011	602	—	—	839	—	—	3 733	—
	2012	52	—	—	735	—	—	30	—
Bulgaria	2010	—	—	—	8	—	—	—	—
	2011	5	—	3	34	—	—	20	—
	2012	—	—	2	2	—	—	10	—
	2013	—	—	—	9	—	—	2	12
Cyprus	2014	—	—	—	°	—	—	—	—
Czech Republic	2014	1 380	—	—	822	—	—	—	1 571
Estonia	2010	8	—	—	°	—	—	7	8
	2011	—	—	5	—	—	—	3	10
	2012	—	—	—	1	—	—	27	—
	2013	—	—	—	1	—	—	1	—
Finland	2011	6	—	—	23	—	—	1	1
	2012	—	—	—	—	—	—	3	—

Country or territory, by region	Year	Acetone (litres)	Anthranilic acid (kilograms)	Ethyl ether (litres)	Hydrochloric acid (litres)	Methyl ethyl ketone (litres)	Piperidine (litres)	Sulphuric acid (litres)	Toluene (litres)
France	2012	—	—	1	—	3 019	—	1	1
Germany	2010	31	—	2	25	—	—	12	19
	2011	17	—	5	77	63	—	8	9
	2012	94	—	97	717	—	—	71	1 164
	2013	12	—	°	15	1	—	48	20
	2014	10	—	—	6	—	—	27	17
Hungary	2010	15	—	2	—	—	—	1	20
	2011	37	—	7	11	—	—	4	6
	2012	35	—	7	11	—	—	—	—
	2013	75	—	2	°	—	—	°	—
	2014	12	—	—	—	—	—	°	—
Latvia	2012	81	—	°	24	—	—	12	—
Netherlands	2010	1 434	—	—	6 178	375	—	522	942
	2011	6 485	—	—	8 429	—	—	12 404	—
	2012	1 245	—	—	4 567	—	—	2 020	—
	2013	—	—	—	19 988	—	—	8 165	1
	2014	8 510	—	—	13 825	—	—	6 555	—
Poland	2010	—	—	—	—	—	—	61	103
	2011	58	—	4	45	—	—	58	15
	2012	285	—	—	3 575	—	—	148	—
	2013	—	—	—	40	—	—	1 436	—
	2014	130	—	—	8	—	—	11	196
Portugal	2012	°	—	—	—	—	—	—	—
	2013	3	—	—	2	—	—	1	—
Romania	2012	3	—	—	—	—	—	—	—

Country or territory, by region	Year	Acetone (litres)	Anthranilic acid (kilograms)	Ethyl ether (litres)	Hydrochloric acid (litres)	Methyl ethyl ketone (litres)	Piperidine (litres)	Sulphuric acid (litres)	Toluene (litres)
Slovakia	2010	–	–	–	4	–	–	–	32
	2011	3	–	–	13	–	–	–	28
	2012	1	–	–	2	–	–	–	20
	2013	–	–	–	8	–	–	–	6
	2014	1	–	1	10	–	–	3	18
Spain	2010	442	–	66	55	43	–	35	4
	2011	1	–	°	1	1	50	1	°
	2012	425	–	287	990	123	–	30	33
	2013	1 190	–	297	490	2 197	–	1 086 979	11 511 987
	2014	85	–	20	159	1	–	1	2
Sweden	2011	–	°	–	–	–	–	–	–
United Kingdom	2010	–	–	–	1	–	–	–	–
	2012	–	–	1	–	385	–	–	–
	2013	–	–	21	–	–	–	20	–
Regional total	**2010**	**23 211**	**0**	**77**	**119 357**	**552**	**0**	**113 752**	**27 394**
	2011	**9 028**	**0**	**574**	**34 127**	**1 770**	**0**	**298 054**	**4 401**
	2012	**12 549**	**0**	**9 635**	**12 859**	**4 266**	**50**	**97 087**	**21 343**
	2013	**2 446**	**0**	**299**	**23 621**	**2 197**	**0**	**1 108 049**	**11 512 633**
	2014	**10 221**	**0**	**21**	**14 851**	**1**	**0**	**6 724**	**1 878**
Oceania									
Australia	2010	54	–	30	214	°	–	278	25
	2011	51	–	1	88	–	–	9	14
	2012	130	–	–	112	16	–	62	83
New Zealand	2010	200	–	6	752	134	–	244	1 434
	2011	203	–	–	308	26	–	28	476
	2012	93	–	–	137	–	–	10	682
	2013	108	–	–	263	13	–	74	835

Country or territory, by region	Year	Acetone (litres)	Anthranilic acid (kilograms)	Ethyl ether (litres)	Hydrochloric acid (litres)	Methyl ethyl ketone (litres)	Piperidine (litres)	Sulphuric acid (litres)	Toluene (litres)
Regional total									
	2010	254	0	36	966	134	0	522	1 459
	2011	254	0	1	396	26	0	37	490
	2012	223	0	0	249	16	0	72	765
	2013	108	0	0	263	13	0	74	835
World total									
	2010	846 973	0	48 683	793 226	86 894	90	1 042 622	125 873
	2011	696 666	0	20 970	679 785	7 343	12	2 040 787	142 307
	2012	986 216	0	60 854	504 165	11 069	257	512 447	126 932
	2013	1 038 127	490 302	43 708	2 332 545	9 264	59	4 146 274	11 749 436
	2014	936 708	816	11 585	3 571 781	8 412	57	7 888 633	2 945 567

[a] The exact quantity of the seizures was not specified.

[b] For statistical purposes, the data for China do not include those for the Hong Kong Special Administrative Region (SAR) of China and the Macao SAR of China.

[c] Reported on form B: annual estimates of requirements of narcotic drugs, manufacture of synthetic drugs, opium production and cultivation of the opium poppy for purposes other than opium production.

Annex IX

Submission of information by Governments on licit trade in, uses of and requirements for substances in Tables I and II of the 1988 Convention for the years 2010-2014

Governments of the countries and territories indicated have provided information on licit trade in, uses of and requirements for substances in Tables I and II of the United Nations Convention against Illicit Traffic in Narcotic Drugs and Psychotropic Substances of 1988 on form D for the years 2010-2014. That information was requested in accordance with Economic and Social Council resolution 1995/20. Details may be made available on a case-by-case basis, subject to confidentiality of data.

Notes: The names of non-metropolitan territories and special administrative regions are in italics.

"X" signifies that relevant information was submitted on form D.

Country or territory	2010		2011		2012		2013		2014	
	Trade	Uses and/or require-ments	Trade	Uses and/or require-ments	Trade	Uses and/or require-ments	Trade	Uses and/or require-ments	Trade	Uses and/or require-ments
Afghanistan					X	X	X	X	X	X
Albania	X	X	X	X	X	X	X	X	X	X
Algeria	X	X	X	X	X	X	X	X	X	X
Andorra					X	X	X	X		
Angola										
Anguilla										
Antigua and Barbuda										
Argentina	X	X	X	X	X	X	X	X	X	X
Armenia	X	X	X	X	X	X	X	X	X	X
Aruba										
Ascension Island										
Australia	X	X	X	X	X	X	X	X	X	X
Austria[a]	X	X	X	X	X	X	X	X	X	X
Azerbaijan	X	X	X	X	X	X	X	X	X	X
Bahamas										
Bahrain	X									
Bangladesh	X	X	X	X	X	X	X	X	X	X
Barbados							X	X		
Belarus	X	X	X	X	X	X	X	X	X	X
Belgium[a]	X	X	X	X	X	X	X	X	X	X
Belize							X	X		
Benin	X	X	X	X	X	X			X	X
Bermuda										
Bhutan	X	X	X	X	X	X			X	X
Bolivia (Plurinational State of)	X	X	X	X	X	X	X	X	X	X

Country or territory	2010		2011		2012		2013		2014	
	Trade	Uses and/or require-ments	Trade	Uses and/or require-ments	Trade	Uses and/or require-ments	Trade	Uses and/or require-ments	Trade	Uses and/or require-ments
Bosnia and Herzegovina			X	X	X	X	X	X	X	X
Botswana										
Brazil	X	X			X	X	X	X	X	X
British Virgin Islands										
Brunei Darussalam	X	X	X	X	X	X	X	X	X	X
Bulgaria[a]	X	X	X		X	X	X	X	X	X
Burkina Faso			X	X						
Burundi										
Cabo Verde										
Cambodia	X	X			X		X	X		X
Cameroon			X		X	X				
Canada	X	X	X	X	X	X	X	X		
Cayman Islands										
Central African Republic										
Chad										
Chile	X	X	X	X	X	X	X	X	X	X
China	X	X	X	X	X	X	X	X	X	X
China, Hong Kong SAR	X	X			X	X	X	X		
China, Macao SAR	X	X			X	X	X	X	X	X
Christmas Island			X	X			X			
Cocos (Keeling) Islands										
Colombia	X	X	X	X	X	X	X	X	X	X
Comoros										
Congo										
Cook Islands			X	X						
Costa Rica	X	X	X	X	X	X	X	X	X	X
Côte d'Ivoire	X	X	X	X	X	X	X	X	X	X
Croatia[a]	X		X		X	X	X	X	X	X
Cuba	X	X	X	X						
Curaçao[b]	X	X	X	X	X	X	X	X	X	X
Cyprus[a]	X	X	X	X	X	X	X	X	X	X
Czech Republic[a]	X	X	X	X	X	X	X	X	X	X
Democratic People's Republic of Korea		X		X		X		X		
Democratic Republic of the Congo	X		X	X	X	X	X		X	X
Denmark[a]	X		X		X	X	X		X	X
Djibouti										
Dominica										
Dominican Republic	X	X					X	X	X	X

Country or territory	2010		2011		2012		2013		2014	
	Trade	Uses and/or require-ments	Trade	Uses and/or require-ments	Trade	Uses and/or require-ments	Trade	Uses and/or require-ments	Trade	Uses and/or require-ments
Ecuador	X	X	X	X	X	X	X	X	X	X
Egypt	X	X	X	X	X	X	X	X	X	X
El Salvador	X	X	X	X	X	X	X	X	X	X
Equatorial Guinea										
Eritrea	X	X	X	X	X	X				
Estonia[a]	X	X	X	X	X	X		X	X	X
Ethiopia			X	X	X	X	X	X		
Falkland Islands (Malvinas)	X	X	X	X	X	X	X	X	X	X
Fiji			X	X						
Finland[a]	X	X	X	X	X	X	X	X	X	X
France[a]	X	X	X	X	X	X	X	X	X	X
French Polynesia										
Gabon										
Gambia							X	X		
Georgia	X	X	X	X	X	X	X	X	X	X
Germany[a]	X	X	X	X	X	X	X	X	X	X
Ghana	X	X	X	X	X	X	X	X	X	X
Gibraltar										
Greece[a]	X	X	X	X	X	X	X	X	X	X
Grenada										
Guatemala	X	X			X	X	X	X	X	X
Guinea										
Guinea-Bissau										
Guyana		X							X	X
Haiti	X	X	X	X						
Holy See										
Honduras			X	X	X	X	X	X		
Hungary[a]	X	X	X	X	X	X	X	X	X	X
Iceland	X	X	X	X	X	X	X	X	X	X
India	X	X	X	X	X	X	X	X		
Indonesia	X	X	X	X	X	X	X	X	X	X
Iran (Islamic Republic of)	X	X					X	X	X	X
Iraq	X	X	X	X						
Ireland[a]	X	X	X	X	X	X	X	X	X	X
Israel	X	X	X	X	X	X	X	X	X	X
Italy[a]	X	X	X	X	X	X	X	X	X	X
Jamaica	X	X					X	X	X	
Japan	X	X	X	X	X	X	X	X	X	X
Jordan	X	X	X	X	X	X	X	X	X	X

Country or territory	2010		2011		2012		2013		2014	
	Trade	Uses and/or require-ments	Trade	Uses and/or require-ments	Trade	Uses and/or require-ments	Trade	Uses and/or require-ments	Trade	Uses and/or require-ments
Kazakhstan	X	X	X	X			X	X		
Kenya	X	X								
Kiribati										
Kuwait					X	X	X	X		
Kyrgyzstan	X	X	X	X	X	X	X	X	X	X
Lao People's Democratic Republic	X	X	X	X	X	X	X	X	X	
Latvia[a]	X	X	X	X	X	X	X	X	X	X
Lebanon	X	X	X	X	X	X	X	X	X	X
Lesotho										X
Liberia			X							
Libya										
Liechtenstein[c]										
Lithuania[a]	X	X	X	X		X	X	X	X	X
Luxembourg[a]	X									
Madagascar	X	X					X	X		
Malawi										
Malaysia	X	X	X	X	X	X	X	X	X	X
Maldives	X	X	X	X	X	X	X	X		
Mali							X	X		
Malta[a]	X	X	X	X		X	X	X	X	X
Marshall Islands										
Mauritania										
Mauritius	X	X	X	X	X	X				
Mexico	X	X	X	X	X	X	X	X	X	X
Micronesia (Federated States of)							X	X		
Monaco										
Mongolia	X	X	X		X	X	X			
Montenegro	X	X	X	X	X	X	X	X	X	X
Montserrat		X			X	X	X	X	X	X
Morocco	X	X	X	X	X	X	X	X		
Mozambique	X	X							X	
Myanmar	X	X	X	X	X	X	X	X	X	X
Namibia										
Nauru										
Nepal							X	X	X	X
Netherlands[a]	X	X	X	X	X	X	X	X	X	X
New Caledonia										
New Zealand	X	X	X	X	X	X	X	X		

Country or territory	2010 Trade	2010 Uses and/or require-ments	2011 Trade	2011 Uses and/or require-ments	2012 Trade	2012 Uses and/or require-ments	2013 Trade	2013 Uses and/or require-ments	2014 Trade	2014 Uses and/or require-ments
Nicaragua	X	X	X	X	X	X	X	X	X	X
Niger										
Nigeria			X	X	X	X	X	X		
Niue										
Norfolk Island										
Norway	X	X			X	X				
Oman									X	X
Pakistan	X	X	X	X	X	X	X	X	X	X
Palau										
Panama	X	X	X	X	X	X	X	X	X	X
Papua New Guinea										
Paraguay	X		X	X						
Peru	X	X	X	X	X	X	X	X	X	X
Philippines	X	X	X	X	X	X	X	X	X	X
Poland[a]	X	X	X	X	X	X	X	X	X	X
Portugal[a]	X		X		X		X	X	X	X
Qatar			X	X			X	X		
Republic of Korea	X	X	X	X	X	X	X	X	X	X
Republic of Moldova	X	X	X	X	X	X	X	X	X	X
Romania[a]	X	X	X	X	X	X	X	X	X	X
Russian Federation	X	X	X	X	X	X	X	X	X	X
Rwanda										
Saint Helena			X	X						
Saint Kitts and Nevis										
Saint Lucia					X	X	X	X	X	X
Saint Vincent and the Grenadines					X	X	X	X	X	X
Samoa					X	X				
San Marino										
Sao Tome and Principe										
Saudi Arabia	X		X		X		X	X	X	X
Senegal	X						X	X	X	X
Serbia	X	X	X	X	X	X	X	X		
Seychelles			X	X	X	X				
Sierra Leone										
Singapore	X	X	X	X	X	X	X	X	X	X
Sint Maarten[b]										
Slovakia[a]	X	X	X	X	X	X	X	X	X	X
Slovenia[a]	X	X	X	X	X	X	X	X	X	X

Country or territory	2010		2011		2012		2013		2014	
	Trade	Uses and/or require-ments	Trade	Uses and/or require-ments	Trade	Uses and/or require-ments	Trade	Uses and/or require-ments	Trade	Uses and/or require-ments
Solomon Islands										
Somalia										
South Africa							X	X		
South Sudan[d]										
Spain[a]	X	X	X	X	X	X	X	X	X	X
Sri Lanka	X		X	X	X	X	X	X	X	
Sudan									X	X
Suriname										
Swaziland										
Sweden[a]	X	X	X	X	X	X	X	X	X	X
Switzerland	X	X	X	X	X	X	X	X	X	X
Syrian Arab Republic	X	X			X	X	X	X		
Tajikistan	X	X	X	X	X	X	X	X		
Thailand	X	X	X	X	X	X	X	X	X	X
The former Yugoslav Republic of Macedonia	X	X								
Timor-Leste										
Togo					X	X				
Tonga										
Trinidad and Tobago	X	X	X	X	X	X	X	X	X	X
Tristan da Cunha										
Tunisia	X	X	X	X	X	X	X	X	X	X
Turkey	X	X	X	X	X	X	X	X	X	X
Turkmenistan					X	X	X	X	X	X
Turks and Caicos Islands										
Tuvalu			X	X						
Uganda	X	X	X	X	X	X	X	X	X	X
Ukraine	X	X	X	X	X	X	X	X		
United Arab Emirates	X	X	X	X	X	X	X	X	X	X
United Kingdom[a]	X	X	X	X	X	X			X	X
United Republic of Tanzania	X	X	X	X	X	X	X	X	X	X
United States of America	X	X	X	X	X	X	X	X	X	X
Uruguay	X	X	X	X	X	X	X	X	X	X
Uzbekistan	X	X	X	X	X	X	X	X	X	X
Vanuatu			X	X						
Venezuela (Bolivarian Republic of)	X	X	X	X	X	X	X	X	X	X
Viet Nam	X	X	X	X	X	X	X	X	X	X
Wallis and Futuna Islands										
Yemen	X		X	X	X	X				

Country or territory	2010 Trade	2010 Uses and/or require-ments	2011 Trade	2011 Uses and/or require-ments	2012 Trade	2012 Uses and/or require-ments	2013 Trade	2013 Uses and/or require-ments	2014 Trade	2014 Uses and/or require-ments
Zambia									X	X
Zimbabwe	X	X		X			X	X	X	X
Total number of Governments that submitted form D	**123**	**115**	**120**	**114**	**120**	**120**	**127**	**125**	**108**	**106**
Total number of Governments requested to provide information	**213**	**213**	**213**	**213**	**213**	**213**	**213**	**213**	**213**	**213**

[a] State member of the European Union.

[b] The Netherlands Antilles was dissolved on 10 October 2010, resulting in two new constituent entities, Curaçao and Sint Maarten.

[c] The Government of Switzerland includes on form D licit trade data for Liechtenstein.

[d] By its resolution 65/308 of 14 July 2011, the General Assembly decided to admit South Sudan to membership in the United Nations.

Annex X

Governments that have requested pre-export notifications pursuant to article 12, paragraph 10 (a), of the 1988 Convention

1.   Governments of all exporting countries and territories are reminded that it is an obligation to provide pre-export notifications to Governments that have requested them, pursuant to article 12, paragraph 10 (a), of the United Nations Convention against Illicit Traffic in Narcotic Drugs and Psychotropic Substances of 1988, which provides that:

> "upon request to the Secretary-General by the interested Party, each Party from whose territory a substance in Table I is to be exported shall ensure that, prior to such export, the following information is supplied by its competent authorities to the competent authorities of the importing country:
>
> "(i)   Name and address of the exporter and importer and, when available, the consignee;
>
> "(ii)   Name of the substance in Table I;
>
> "(iii) Quantity of the substance to be exported;
>
> "(iv) Expected point of entry and expected date of dispatch;
>
> "(v)   Any other information which is mutually agreed upon by the Parties."

2.   Governments that have requested pre-export notifications under the above provisions are listed in the table below in alphabetical order, followed by the substance (or substances) to which the provisions apply and the date of notification of the request transmitted by the Secretary-General to Governments. The information is current as at 1 November 2015.

3.   Governments may wish to note the possibility of requesting that a pre-export notification for all substances listed in Table II of the 1988 Convention be sent as well.

Notifying Government	Substances to which the pre-export notification requirement applies	Date of communication to Governments by the Secretary-General
Afghanistan[a]	All substances included in Tables I and II	13 July 2010
Algeria[a]	All substances included in Tables I and II	10 October 2013
Antigua and Barbuda[a]	All substances included in Tables I and II	5 May 2000
Argentina	All substances included in Table I	19 November 1999
Armenia[a]	All substances included in Tables I and II[b,c]	4 July 2013
Australia[a]	All substances included in Tables I and II	12 February 2010
Austria	All substances included in Table I	19 May 2000[d]
Azerbaijan[a]	All substances included in Tables I and II	21 January 2011
Bangladesh[a]	All substances included in Tables I and II	12 May 2015
Barbados[a]	All substances included in Tables I and II[b,c]	24 October 2013
Belarus[e]	Acetic anhydride, ephedrine, potassium permanganate and pseudoephedrine	12 October 2000
Belgium	All substances included in Table I	19 May 2000
Benin[a]	All substances included in Tables I and II	4 February 2000

Notifying Government	Substances to which the pre-export notification requirement applies	Date of communication to Governments by the Secretary-General
Bolivia (Plurinational State of)[a]	Acetic anhydride, acetone, ethyl ether, hydrochloric acid, potassium permanganate and sulphuric acid	12 November 2001
Brazil[a]	All substances included in Tables I and II	15 October and 15 December 1999
Bulgaria	All substances included in Table I	19 May 2000[d]
Canada[a]	All substances included in Tables I and II	31 October 2005
Cayman Islands[a]	All substances included in Tables I and II	7 September 1998
Chile[a]	All substances included in Tables I and II	19 October 2012
China	Acetic anhydride	20 October 2000
China, Hong Kong SAR[a]	All substances included in Tables I and II	28 December 2012
China, Macao SAR[a]	All substances included in Tables I and II	28 December 2012
Colombia[a]	All substances included in Tables I and II	14 October 1998
Costa Rica[a]	All substances included in Tables I and II	27 September 1999
Côte d'Ivoire[a]	All substances included in Tables I and II	26 June 2013
Croatia	All substances included in Table I	19 May 2000[d]
Cyprus	All substances included in Table I	19 May 2000[d]
Czech Republic	All substances included in Table I	19 May 2000[d]
Denmark	All substances included in Table I	19 May 2000[d]
Dominican Republic[a]	All substances included in Tables I and II	11 September 2002
Ecuador[a]	All substances included in Tables I and II	1 August 1996
Egypt[a]	All substances included in Table I and acetone	3 December 2004
El Salvador[a]	All substances included in Tables I and II	29 July 2010
Estonia	All substances included in Table I	19 May 2000
Ethiopia[a]	All substances included in Tables I and II	17 December 1999
Finland	All substances included in Table I	19 May 2000[d]
France	All substances included in Table I	19 May 2000[d]
Germany	All substances included in Table I	19 May 2000[d]
Ghana[a]	All substances included in Tables I and II	26 February 2010
Greece	All substances included in Table I	19 May 2000[d]
Haiti[a]	All substances included in Tables I and II	20 June 2002
Hungary	All substances included in Table I	19 May 2000[d]
India[a]	All substances included in Tables I and II	23 March 2000
Indonesia[a]	Acetic anhydride, N-acetylanthranilic acid, anthranilic acid, ephedrine, ergometrine, ergotamine, isosafrole, 3,4-methylenedioxyphenyl-2-propanone, phenylacetic acid, 1-phenyl-2-propanone, piperonal, pseudoephedrine and safrole	18 February 2000
Iraq[a]	All substances included in Tables I and II[b,c]	31 July 2013
Ireland	All substances included in Table I	19 May 2000[d]
Italy	All substances included in Table I	19 May 2000[d]
Jamaica	All substances included in Table I[b,c]	4 July 2013
Japan	All substances included in Table I	17 December 1999
Jordan[a]	All substances included in Tables I and II	15 December 1999
Kazakhstan[a]	All substances included in Tables I and II	15 August 2003
Kenya[a]	All substances included in Tables I and II[b,c]	10 October 2013
Kyrgyzstan[a]	All substances included in Tables I and II[b,c]	21 October 2013

Notifying Government	Substances to which the pre-export notification requirement applies	Date of communication to Governments by the Secretary-General
Latvia	All substances included in Table I	19 May 2000[d]
Lebanon[a]	All substances included in Tables I and II	14 June 2002
Libya[a]	All substances included in Tables I and II[b,c]	21 August 2013
Lithuania	All substances included in Table I	19 May 2000[d]
Luxembourg	All substances included in Table I	19 May 2000[d]
Madagascar[a]	All substances included in Tables I and II	31 March 2003
Malaysia[a]	All substances included in Table I,[b] anthranilic acid, ethyl ether and piperidine	21 August 1998
Maldives[a]	All substances included in Tables I and II	6 April 2005
Malta	All substances included in Table I	19 May 2000[d]
Mexico[a]	All substances included in Tables I and II	6 April 2005
Micronesia (Federal States of)[a]	All substances included in Tables I and II[b,c]	11 February 2014
Netherlands	All substances included in Table I	19 May 2000[d]
New Zealand[a]	All substances included in Tables I and II[b,c]	3 April 2014
Nicaragua[a]	All substances included in Tables I and II	8 January 2014
Nigeria[a]	All substances included in Tables I and II	28 February 2000
Norway[a]	All substances included in Table I,[c] anthranilic acid, ethyl ether and piperidine	17 December 2013
Oman[a]	All substances included in Tables I and II	16 April 2007
Pakistan[a]	All substances included in Tables I and II	12 November 2001 and 6 March 2013
Panama	Ephedrine, ergometrine, ergotamine, norephedrine and pseudoephedrine	14 August 2013
Paraguay[a]	All substances included in Tables I and II	3 February 2000
Peru[a]	Acetic anhydride, acetone, ephedrine, ergometrine, ergotamine, ethyl ether, hydrochloric acid, lysergic acid, methyl ethyl ketone, norephedrine, potassium permanganate, pseudoephedrine, sulphuric acid and toluene	27 September 1999
Philippines[a]	All substances included in Tables I and II	16 April 1999
Poland	All substances included in Table I	19 May 2000[d]
Portugal	All substances included in Table I	19 May 2000[d]
Qatar[a]	All substances included in Tables I and II[b,c]	16 July 2013
Republic of Korea[a]	All substances included in Table I and acetone	3 June 2008
Republic of Moldova[a]	All substances included in Tables I and II[b,c]	29 December 1998 and 8 November 2013
Romania	All substances included in Table I	19 May 2000[d]
Russian Federation[a]	Acetic anhydride, ephedrine, ergometrine, ergotamine, 3,4-methylenedioxyphenyl-2-propanone, norephedrine, phenylacetic acid, 1-phenyl-2-propanone, potassium permanganate, pseudoephedrine and all substances included in Table II	21 February 2000
Saint Vincent and the Grenadines[a]	All substances included in Tables I and II[b,c]	16 July 2013
Saudi Arabia[a]	All substances included in Tables I and II	18 October 1998
Sierra Leone[a]	All substances included in Tables I and II[b,c]	5 July 2013
Singapore	All substances included in Table I	5 May 2000
Slovakia	All substances included in Table I	19 May 2000[d]
Slovenia	All substances included in Table I	19 May 2000[d]
South Africa[a]	All substances included in Table I and anthranilic acid	11 August 1999

Notifying Government	Substances to which the pre-export notification requirement applies	Date of communication to Governments by the Secretary-General
Spain	All substances included in Table I	19 May 2000[d]
Sri Lanka	All substances included in Table I	19 November 1999
Sudan	All substances included in Tables I and II	6 May 2015
Sweden	All substances included in Table I	19 May 2000[d]
Switzerland	All substances included in Table I	25 March 2013
Syrian Arab Republic[a]	All substances included in Tables I and II	24 October 2013
Tajikistan[a]	All substances included in Tables I and II	7 February 2000
Thailand[a]	All substances included in Table I (except potassium permanganate) and anthranilic acid[b]	18 October 2010
Togo[a]	All substances included in Tables I and II	6 August 2013
Tonga[a]	All substances included in Tables I and II[b,c]	4 July 2013
Trinidad and Tobago[a]	All substances included in Tables I and II[b,c]	15 August 2013
Turkey[a]	All substances included in Tables I and II	2 November 1995
Uganda[a]	All substances included in Tables I and II[b,c]	6 May 2014
United Arab Emirates[a]	All substances included in Tables I[b] and II	26 September 1995
United Kingdom	All substances included in Table I	19 May 2000[d]
United Republic of Tanzania[a]	All substances included in Tables I and II	10 December 2002
United States of America	Acetic anhydride, ephedrine and pseudoephedrine	2 June 1995 and 19 January 2001
Venezuela (Bolivarian Republic of)[a]	All substances included in Tables I and II	27 March 2000
Yemen[a]	All substances included in Tables I and II	6 May 2014
Zimbabwe[a]	All substances included in Tables I and II[b,c]	4 July 2013
European Union (on behalf of all its States members)[f]	All substances included in Table I	19 May 2000[d]

Note: The names of territories are in italics.

[a] The Secretary-General has informed all Governments of the request of the notifying Government to receive a pre-export notification for some or all substances listed in Table II of the 1988 Convention as well.

[b] Government requested to receive pre-export notifications for pharmaceutical preparations containing ephedrine and pseudoephedrine as well.

[c] Government requested to receive pre-export notifications for safrole-rich oils as well.

[d] On 19 May 2000, the Secretary-General communicated to Governments the request by the European Commission, on behalf of the States members of the European Union, to receive pre-export notifications for the substances indicated.

[e] Not yet notified by the Secretary-General, as, in a subsequent communication, the Government of Belarus requested the Secretary-General to suspend such notification until a national mechanism to receive and process pre-export notifications was established.

[f] Austria, Belgium, Bulgaria, Croatia, Cyprus, Czech Republic, Denmark, Estonia, Finland, France, Germany, Greece, Hungary, Ireland, Italy, Latvia, Lithuania, Luxembourg, Malta, Netherlands, Poland, Portugal, Romania, Slovakia, Slovenia, Spain, Sweden and United Kingdom of Great Britain and Northern Ireland.

Annex XI

Licit uses of the substances in Tables I and II of the 1988 Convention

Knowledge of the most common licit uses of substances in Tables I and II of the United Nations Convention against Illicit Traffic in Narcotic Drugs and Psychotropic Substances of 1988, including the processes and end products in which the substances may be used, is essential for the verification of the legitimacy of orders or shipments. The most common licit uses of those substances reported to the International Narcotics Control Board are as follows:

Substance	Licit uses
Acetic anhydride	Acetylating and dehydrating agent used in the chemical and pharmaceutical industries for the manufacture of cellulose acetate, for textile sizing agents and cold bleaching activators, for polishing metals and for the production of brake fluids, dyes and explosives
Acetone	As a common solvent and intermediate for a variety of substances in the chemical and pharmaceutical industries, including plastics, paints, lubricants, varnishes and cosmetics; also used in the manufacture of other solvents, such as chloroform
N-Acetylanthranilic acid	Used in the manufacture of pharmaceuticals, plastics and fine chemicals
Anthranilic acid	Chemical intermediate used in the manufacture of dyes, pharmaceuticals and perfumes; also used in the preparation of bird and insect repellents
Ephedrine	Used in the manufacture of bronchodilators (cough medicines)
Ergometrine	Used in the treatment of migraine and as an oxytocic in obstetrics
Ergotamine	Used in the treatment of migraine and as an oxytocic in obstetrics
Ethyl ether	Commonly used solvent in chemical laboratories and in the chemical and pharmaceutical industries; mainly used as an extractant for fats, oils, waxes and resins; also used for the manufacture of munitions, plastics and perfumes and, in medicine, as a general anaesthetic
Hydrochloric acid	Used in the production of chlorides and hydrochlorides, for the neutralization of basic systems and as a catalyst and solvent in organic synthesis
Isosafrole	Used in the manufacture of piperonal; to modify "oriental perfumes"; to strengthen soap perfumes; in small quantities, together with methyl salicylate, in root beer and sarsaparilla flavours; and as a pesticide
Lysergic acid	Used in organic synthesis
3,4-Methylenedioxyphenyl-2-propanone	Used in the manufacture of piperonal and other perfume components
Methyl ethyl ketone	Common solvent; used in the manufacture of coatings, solvents, degreasing agents, lacquers, resins and smokeless powders
Norephedrine	Used in the manufacture of nasal decongestants and appetite suppressants

Substance	Licit uses
Phenylacetic acid	Used in the chemical and pharmaceutical industries for the manufacture of phenylacetate esters, amphetamine and some derivatives; also used for the synthesis of penicillins and in fragrance applications and cleaning solutions
alpha-Phenylacetoacetonitrile	None, except — in small amounts — for research, development and laboratory analytical purposes
1-Phenyl-2-propanone	Used in the chemical and pharmaceutical industries for the manufacture of amphetamine, methamphetamine and some derivatives; also used for the synthesis of propylhexedrine
Piperidine	Commonly used solvent and reagent in chemical laboratories and in the chemical and pharmaceutical industries; also used in the manufacture of rubber products and plastics
Piperonal	Used in perfumery, in cherry and vanilla flavours, in organic synthesis and as a component for mosquito repellent
Potassium permanganate	Important reagent in analytical and synthetic organic chemistry; used in bleaching applications, disinfectants, antibacterials and antifungal agents and in water purification
Pseudoephedrine	Used in the manufacture of bronchodilators and nasal decongestants
Safrole	Used in perfumery, for example in the manufacture of piperonal, and for denaturing fats in soap manufacture
Sulphuric acid	Used in the production of sulphates; as an acidic oxidizer; as a dehydrating and purifying agent; for the neutralization of alkaline solutions; as a catalyst in organic synthesis; in the manufacture of fertilizers, explosives, dyestuffs and paper; and as a component of drain and metal cleaners, anti-rust compounds and automobile battery fluids
Toluene	Industrial solvent; used in the manufacture of explosives, dyes, coatings and other organic substances and as a gasoline additive

About the International Narcotics Control Board

The International Narcotics Control Board (INCB) is an independent and quasi-judicial control organ, established by treaty, for monitoring the implementation of the international drug control treaties. It had predecessors under the former drug control treaties as far back as the time of the League of Nations.

Composition

INCB consists of 13 members who are elected by the Economic and Social Council and who serve in their personal capacity, not as Government representatives. Three members with medical, pharmacological or pharmaceutical experience are elected from a list of persons nominated by the World Health Organization (WHO) and 10 members are elected from a list of persons nominated by Governments. Members of the Board are persons who, by their competence, impartiality and disinterestedness, command general confidence. The Council, in consultation with INCB, makes all arrangements necessary to ensure the full technical independence of the Board in carrying out its functions. INCB has a secretariat that assists it in the exercise of its treaty-related functions. The INCB secretariat is an administrative entity of the United Nations Office on Drugs and Crime, but it reports solely to the Board on matters of substance. INCB closely collaborates with the Office in the framework of arrangements approved by the Council in its resolution 1991/48. INCB also cooperates with other international bodies concerned with drug control, including not only the Council and its Commission on Narcotic Drugs, but also the relevant specialized agencies of the United Nations, particularly WHO. It also cooperates with bodies outside the United Nations system, especially the International Criminal Police Organization (INTERPOL) and the World Customs Organization.

Functions

The functions of INCB are laid down in the following treaties: the Single Convention on Narcotic Drugs of 1961 as amended by the 1972 Protocol; the Convention on Psychotropic Substances of 1971; and the United Nations Convention against Illicit Traffic in Narcotic Drugs and Psychotropic Substances of 1988. Broadly speaking, INCB deals with the following:

(a)   As regards the licit manufacture of, trade in and use of drugs, INCB endeavours, in cooperation with Governments, to ensure that adequate supplies of drugs are available for medical and scientific uses and that the diversion of drugs from licit sources to illicit channels does not occur. INCB also monitors Governments' control over chemicals used in the illicit manufacture of drugs and assists them in preventing the diversion of those chemicals into the illicit traffic;

(b)   As regards the illicit manufacture of, trafficking in and use of drugs, INCB identifies weaknesses in national and international control systems and contributes to correcting such situations. INCB is also responsible for assessing chemicals used in the illicit manufacture of drugs, in order to determine whether they should be placed under international control.

In the discharge of its responsibilities, INCB:

(a)   Administers a system of estimates for narcotic drugs and a voluntary assessment system for psychotropic substances and monitors licit activities involving drugs through a statistical returns system, with a view to assisting Governments in achieving, inter alia, a balance between supply and demand;

(b)   Monitors and promotes measures taken by Governments to prevent the diversion of substances frequently used in the illicit manufacture of narcotic drugs and psychotropic substances and assesses such substances to determine whether there is a need for changes in the scope of control of Tables I and II of the 1988 Convention;

(c)   Analyses information provided by Governments, United Nations bodies, specialized agencies or other competent international organizations, with a view to ensuring that the provisions of the international drug control treaties are adequately carried out by Governments, and recommends remedial measures;

(d)   Maintains a permanent dialogue with Governments to assist them in complying with their obligations under the international drug control treaties and, to that end, recommends, where appropriate, technical or financial assistance to be provided.

INCB is called upon to ask for explanations in the event of apparent violations of the treaties, to propose appropriate remedial measures to Governments that are not fully applying the provisions of the treaties or are encountering difficulties in applying them and, where necessary, to assist Governments in overcoming such difficulties. If, however, INCB notes that the measures necessary to remedy a serious situation have not been taken, it may call the matter to the attention of the parties concerned, the Commission on Narcotic Drugs and the Economic and Social Council. As a last resort, the treaties empower INCB to recommend to parties that they stop importing drugs from a defaulting country, exporting drugs to it or both. In all cases, INCB acts in close cooperation with Governments.

INCB assists national administrations in meeting their obligations under the conventions. To that end, it proposes and participates in regional training seminars and programmes for drug control administrators.

Reports

The international drug control treaties require INCB to prepare an annual report on its work. The annual report contains an analysis of the drug control situation worldwide so that Governments are kept aware of existing and potential situations that may endanger the objectives of the international drug control treaties. INCB draws the attention of Governments to gaps and weaknesses in national control and in treaty compliance; it also makes suggestions and recommendations for improvements at both the national and international levels. The annual report is based on information provided by Governments to INCB, United Nations entities and other organizations. It also uses information provided through other international organizations, such as INTERPOL and the World Customs Organization, as well as regional organizations.

The annual report of INCB is supplemented by detailed technical reports. They contain data on the licit movement of narcotic drugs and psychotropic substances required for medical and scientific purposes, together with an analysis of those data by INCB. Those data are required for the proper functioning of the system of control over the licit movement of narcotic drugs and psychotropic substances, including preventing their diversion to illicit channels. Moreover, under the provisions of article 12 of the 1988 Convention, INCB reports annually to the Commission on Narcotic Drugs on the implementation of that article. That report, which gives an account of the results of the monitoring of precursors and of the chemicals frequently used in the illicit manufacture of narcotic drugs and psychotropic substances, is also published as a supplement to the annual report.

www.ingramcontent.com/pod-product-compliance
Lightning Source LLC
Chambersburg PA
CBHW080840270326
41926CB00018B/4102